The
NATURAL WONDERS
of the
BRITISH ISLES

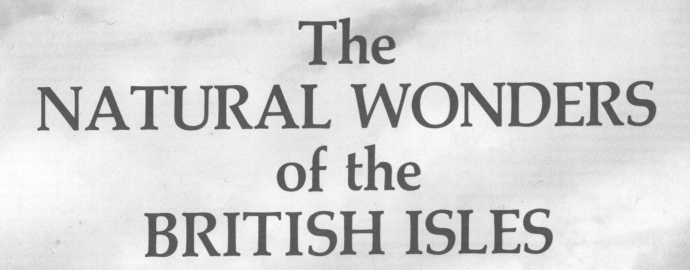

The
NATURAL WONDERS
of the
BRITISH ISLES

Charles Walker

Orbis Publishing — London

Right: Malham Cove in the snow.

Previous page: The basalt columns and pavements on the island of Staffa, Scotland.

First published in Great Britain by Orbis Publishing Limited, London 1982.

Printed in Hong Kong by South China Printing Co.

ISBN: 0-85613-427-9

Contents

Introduction

Left: The entrance to Fingal's cave on the Hebridean island of Staffa, a wonder of extruded basalts.

Far left and below: Remains of the ancient land-bridge which connected England to the Continent, on the beach at Bexhill.

The geological history of Britain's making is still to be seen in her landscapes. Long ago the British Isles were a mere promontory of Europe, with a wide river, which was eventually to become the Thames and the Rhine, flowing through the lowlands. Then, there was perhaps a slight shift of the earth's axis, a movement of the earth's crust, and slowly the lands started to drift apart. The Baltic Sea and the North Sea were created as the waters poured in. A little while later these seas swept through and across the area which we now call the English Channel, and started to carve out the white cliffs of Dover.

The marks of these cataclysms can be seen in many places. For example, monumental shifts are evident at the quiet seaside resort of Bexhill, where a low tide will reveal delicate turrets of rock castles, fossil remains of the land-bridge which long ago connected our island to the European mainland. There is a strange poignancy in the feeling that such delicate beauty should be the result of upheavals so vast as to sever lands, displace seas, and create a new history of the world.

The British Isles are provided everywhere with natural wonders which speak of such ancient catastrophes. The island of Staffa in Scotland is the exquisite workmanship of cooling basaltic crusts, echoed on the northern tip of Ireland at the Giant's Causeway. The wild exuberance of Glencoe was born from volcanic thrusts, and is really the vast plug of a ring fault, speaking of upheavals in the earth's crust, just as mighty as those at Dunnottar near Stonehaven, where the energies unleashed were so extraordinary as to twist horizontal stratifications of rock into verticals.

Alongside such titanic furies of nature we see also the results of the persistent and inexorable effects of water, which is ever-present in our water-locked islands. Hidden below the surface of the earth is the perpetual sculpting of cave systems, on the surface the perpetual erosion by rivers and waterfalls. In Yorkshire the caves of White Scar are still being made, and tiny droplets of acidic rains and streams are even now gouging out the deep grykes on the Buttertubs Pass, while, more openly dramatic, the mighty High Force etches at the vertical Great Whin Sill which stretches its granite way across Durham and Northumberland.

The natural formations have all contributed to give each of the distinctive areas of Britain their own peculiar character. One may scarcely think of Scotland without picturing its mountains, which are the land's backbone, with the most prominent vertebra the aloof Ben Nevis to the west, opposed by the massif of the Cairngorms which proliferates to the east. One cannot try to imagine England without bearing in mind that it is the largest part of an island, so that even the name England calls up to the distant traveller images of the chalk cliffs which face against the Continent in ancient defiance. Nor can Ireland be pictured without imagining the contrasts it offers between the elemental furies which have carved her cliffs and the more delicate mould-ings of the sheltered country inland, such as in the Burren. A similar contrast is found in Wales, a country which gives the impression of having been condensed from the mists, with the peaks of Snowdonia and the magnificence of the Welsh waterfalls somehow still unreal and quite clearly still in the making rather than fully made.

And yet Britain is a series of islands, and the four countries are united by their coastlines. In these, so various and so distinctive, is found the real wonder of the British Isles, for the sea has carved fantasies in a bewildering variety of forms along these thousands of miles of chalk, granite, schists, sandstones and basalts. I doubt that anywhere in the world can there be found in so short a compass such a rich variety of cove and cave, of the massive and the delicate, the wild and the serene, as can be found in the coastlines of Britain. The contrasts and variety

are almost beyond belief. Within only hundreds of miles we find the isolated splendour of St John's Cliffs on Hoy in the Orkneys, the undulant Seven Sisters of East Sussex, a whole plethora of savagery along the Cornish coasts which has been a horror to shipping and an ancient delight to pirates, and the exquisite sculptural purity of such coastlines as are to be found near Arbroath. The variety is incredible.

In places where the seas cannot work their sculptural magic the rocks and strata are pushed inland to break their way through surface soils and marls, and these in their turn are moulded by the streaming rains. Left behind are strange sentinels to a different geological time: one such example is a curious chain of rocks which march in a great semi-circle along the valley edge above Forest Drive near Pickering, called the Bridestones, although the link which their name forges with the ancient cult of St Bridget has been lost. The many extraordinary extrusions of granite which push like vertical stratifications into the air are nowhere more beautiful than in the Roche of Cornwall. The French name speaks of the close connection between the south of England and the Continent, recalling also the fairy-tale island off Mount Bay, whose name – St Michael – is identical to that of that other island off the coast of Normandy. Less dramatic

perhaps, and certainly less beautiful, is the unexpected Hemlock Stone, thrusting its distinctive red and black form through the grass base, as though it were a meteorite dropped from space. Yet the natural wonders need not be large, isolated or strange to be impressive. Some of the tiny pebbles on these coastline beaches are just as miraculous as the rocks, islands and sea-stacks. There is, for example, a quiet strand of pebbles in the tiny seaside village of Inverbervie on the eastern coast of Scotland which is a vast treasury of wonders. The pebbles are gems, perfect in form and hue, the smooth conglomerates of rich veins of colour speaking the language of beauty and wonder to everyone on a scale which may be held in the hand.

The choice of wonders, in a land which rejoices in so many and such various ones, is itself a problem, and one which I will touch upon in the separate introductions to the four countries. Yet a greater difficulty is that of setting down in mere words why the chosen ones are special. The finest wonders are almost beyond words: they speak for themselves in such a way as to make words almost irrelevant. When the connoisseur Sir George Beaumont was discussing with the landscape painter John Constable the vexing problem of painting Gor-

Above: A panorama of the Cairngorm range of mountains, with the Cairn Gorm itself to the extreme left. The view is from the west of Loch Morlich.

dale Scar in the Yorkshire Dales, he said that he considered it 'beyond the range of art'. I know exactly what he means, for I have felt this time and time again when faced with attempting to portray and reveal in words the nature of these wonders. Perhaps the best one may do is merely to indicate by means of pictures, and remain silent.

Photographs, then, provide a silent pointing. I have tried to present these images of the magnificence of nature as they may be seen and experienced by ordinary travellers. No trickery has been needed to enhance the beauty and marvel of these places, of course; I have to a

Below: One of the extraordinary rock fantasies at Brimham Rocks on the Yorkshire moors. Some of these outcrops have been worked on by a human hand, making their forms even more bizarre.

Above: One of the Bridestones – eroded land-stacks which range along the valley head above Forest Drive, north of Pickering, Yorkshire.

Right: The free-standing stack called the Hemlock Stone, railed in as though it were some dangerous wild beast. The rails are intended to keep vandals out.

great extent tried to remain quite anonymous as a photographer, and permit them to speak for themselves. Wherever possible, I have restricted myself to recording the sites from the most accessible standpoint, for I have felt that I am merely a guide for those who would wish to follow in my long journey through these lands. Even so, I have found at times that it has been necessary to illustrate a place from a particular position which required dangerous climbs and which I would not suggest the general tourist imitate. For example, in order to illustrate the full stature of the Old Man of Hoy, it was necessary to climb down the nearby cliff-fall: this is not a descent to be recommended to the casual traveller, assuming that the casual traveller is prepared to make the long journey to see the Old Man of Hoy in the first place. Other than such rare examples, however, I have tried to treat each of the photographs as so much reportage, on the basis that they have no need of artifice – they reveal themselves as wonders without needing enhancement by art.

Almost all of the wonders are large. Some are, indeed, too large to photograph in the normal way. At best, a camera may reduce the hundreds of square miles of the Cairngorms into a distant undulation of blue horizon. The Great Whin Sill will not reveal itself to the lens: it may

be recorded only in fragmentary images. The magnificent High Force falls over the Sill itself, and one end of it is seen dipping into the sea at Holy Island. These are extreme examples, of course, but the problem of suggesting scale has been a constant one even with smaller wonders. I have tried to suggest a sense of grandeur and scale without including people, which is the standard photographic solution to the problem of scale. Sometimes the human element does help, as for example in the contrast which the two walkers afford against the Eagle Stone, or the surprising image of a hiker through the waterfall hole at Gordale Scar, for in such cases one is confronted with an element of shock and the scale is immediately perceived. Yet to include too many people in a book of this kind would have the effect of destroying the remote wildness which is so much an integral part of so many natural wonders. The real geological wonders have an element of mystery, a quality of isolation – they are quite 'inhuman' and removed from the everyday world which we so thoughtlessly term the 'real' world.

The majority of guidebooks luxuriate in photographs laden with blue skies. This is all very well for Mediterranean countries, but it would not do justice to the British Isles. The most characteristic thing about Britain is the variability of its weather, and I would therefore have been guilty of distortion had I suggested in my pictures that its skies are always clear, cloudless and blue. In the photographs, therefore, you will find a full range of the British weather – you will, indeed, see something of the elemental forces which formed, and continue to form, so many of the natural wonders – the snows of the Yorkshire moors, the fogs of the Cornish coasts, the mist-laden sullen skies of Wales, the intense rains over Ben Nevis; and, in every part of these four countries, at certain times, those welcome blue skies, and the wonderful sunsets and dawns. This extraordinary variety in the elements and weather is the very magic which weaves light and form around these wonders, and reveals the subtle language of these British Isles which I love.

ENGLAND

PICTURE: HIGH FORCE – SEE PAGE 42

Right: A view westward down the last few miles of Honister Pass.

Below: Honister Pass, looking eastwards, along the highest point. Running alongside the road is a fast-flowing stream with delightful waterfalls on its eastern descent.

Introduction

You feel this sea is no mere liquid element encompassing an island. It is an untamed, unsleeping lioness with her mane forever ruffled, guarding and isolating England.
                                        Nikos Kazantzakis

England is defended by the sea in the east and south and cut off by mountains in the north and west, geographical conditions which to a large extent account for the curious history of this land. The vast lengths of beaches and rugged cliffs, which separate the island from the seas and from the historic threats of those menacing lands beyond them, explain why so many of the English natural wonders are related to the sea. Examples abound: there are rich series of coves and caves such as those at Flamborough in the north-east, the fantastic rock-scapes of Durdle Door and Old Harry Rock to the south, the granite thrusts of Land's End to the furthest west and, of course, the whole series of white cliffs associated with Dover, but really starting well before Beachy Head. Almost obliterated by the works of man at Dover, these white cliffs reassert themselves in all their natural pride at St Margaret's Bay.

Even inland wonders are often the result of the power of water, which eventually returns to the sea. The cliff faces and mountains inland have largely been carved by glaciers – the streamroller power of water turned to ice – which can also create such delicately balanced formations as the beautiful erratics at Norber. Water is carving wonders still, for Great Britain, like the rest of the world, is a sculpture in the making, a continuous creation. The underground rivers at Gordale and Malham work with the same fury, though it is a hidden fury, as the splendid open displays of water power at High Force.

Thus it is mainly the workings of seas and waters which account for the geological wonders of England, which is why those selected are of a different order from those chosen for Scotland and Wales. You find no savage Welsh mountains here, no isolated Scottish lochs and glens. England is geologically and geographically different from the surrounding triad of Scotland, Wales and Ireland, as though each were separated by hundreds of miles of sea, rather than encompassed roughly in one single conglomerate.

What persuades one to choose any particular wonder at the expense of another? Why, for instance, choose Winnats Pass as the outstanding example of a narrow pass, instead of the exquisitely lovely Honister Pass? The choice was made not merely because Winnats is a pass of great beauty, hardly spoiled by the narrow road which runs through it, but because beneath its deceptively smooth green and white slopes there are the most wonderful cave systems in the world, the finest of which is Treak Cavern. With this choice, two wonders are revealed in one – an example of how the outer aspect of a wonder may often hide another one.

Again, why choose Lydford Gorge, as against the other gorges, such as Cheddar, for example? It is the very structure of Lydford, with its great cosmic balance of wonders on either end of the gorge – the dark Devil's Cauldron and the light White Lady Falls – which almost teach an object lesson in the power of nature.

Natural standing stones are spread throughout the English landscape, as are the man-made stone-circles and dolmens. Here again the problem is which to select and which to reject, for there are many, and almost all of them are impressive. The Cheesewring of Bodmin Moor almost selects itself, because of its size and beauty, and also because of its dramatic and unique situation on the edge of a vast quarry, hemmed in by a past written in stones. The choice of the Cheesewring meant that other equally impressive standing-stones could not be included. The Bowder Stone, for example, really a huge boulder which freed itself from the nearby mountain-sides, should perhaps have found its way to these pages, and even the lesser-known eroded Eagle Rock near Culver Ridge – and indeed Culver Ridge itself – could have entered the list.

One of the pleasures of this kind of book is that one can balance the well known against the

lesser known, the public against the private. Many of the wonders recorded here are so famous that they include themselves. It would have been an affront to have ignored the vast display of waters at Gordale Scar, the epic of St Michael's Mount, the ancient magic of Holy Island, and the cave systems of White Scar, since each of these are wonders. Yet I have also chosen one or two of the lesser-known wonders which thrill and perplex me personally with their forms or histories. The erratics and clints of Norber Moor would probably fall into this category. Similarly I have included the leaping falls of the little-known Henhole, isolated in the Cheviot Hills, though surrounded by more famous wonders, such as the Northumberland Forest Park, or the Linhope Spout.

Land's End, where England begins, and the lovely Lizard, where the land dips south, could scarcely have been excluded in a full treatment, yet my own love for this part of Cornwall has persuaded me to point out another wonder which stands between them. This is the beautiful peninsula which bears the curious Logan Stone, balanced like a giant building block upon a half-finished wall. There are, of course, many such rocks throughout the English countryside, but this stone is to me a special delight, because of its placing and its curious history.

The natural wonders I most regret not including are the magnificent ridges of the Roaches in the East Midlands. It is said that wallabies, escaped from a local zoo, have made their homes in these high rocks. Yet, this Australian misplacing aside, the place is a wonder; and, having stood on the tips of these granite facings of the Roaches (a name given to the rocks, it is said, by French prisoners of the Napoleonic Wars, the French *rochers* meaning simply 'rocks'), I know that, had I space enough, they would have been recorded here.

The waterfalls of England did not on the whole exert the same claim as did the waterfalls of Wales: it might well be possible to count the waterfalls in England, but I doubt that anyone could count the waterfalls of Wales. And yet, two of the great wonders of England are waterfalls. The resounding High Force is the most amazing falls I know in the length and breadth of Britain, and Hardraw is the highest clear fall, but scarcely of the broad magnificence and sheer cacophony of High Force. Yet, having included these two, it could well be asked why I did not also include the wide and colourful cataracts of Aysgarth in north Yorkshire, or the meandering stream of Golitha Falls on Bodmin Moor, set against some of the most lovely wooded scenery in England ... Again, I can only defend myself by saying that a choice, by definition, must also exclude: I am only too well aware that another man faced with the same choice might well choose the same number without including half the ones I have chosen from my own collection of favourites.

Buttertubs and Hardraw Force

I found myself suddenly looking down a narrow, circular, limestone chasm or chimney, a crevasse that simply disappeared into the bowels of the earth, vertically.

SPB Mais

The approach to Swaledale is guarded by Hardraw Force, which lies behind the village of Hawes. Entrance to the tourist pathway which leads to the force, or 'waterfall', is by way of a turnstile in the 'Green Dragon' pub, which would be entirely unromantic were it not reminiscent of how the fairyland of CS Lewis was reached by way of a wardrobe.

This guardian of the dales is fed by the River Ure, which rises near Abbotside Common, just inside the Yorkshire boundary, and pours into fame at the great scar of Hardraw. These are the highest unbroken waterfalls in Great Britain: the complete leap is over a hundred feet and is set against a semi-circle of rock strata which make it quite clear that long ago the display of water was even more magnificent than it is today.

Since the rotund stratification of cliff has been eroded by these waters into an alarming overhang, it is possible to walk beneath the falls on a sloping raised ledge which is directly beneath. It is, of course, difficult to avoid the spray from the bouncing waters of the cascade as it splashes into the basin, but this is a walk which any visitor should make at least once: the falls are spectacular when seen from across the basin, but quite awe-inspiring when seen from below the cascade itself.

Beyond Hardraw Scar and the falls lies Swaledale, without any doubt the most lovely of the Yorkshire Dales, with a wild beauty which is the result of the giant gouging of glacial ice. There is something austere about these dales, as though the work of the ice is somehow not yet finished, and one has the impression that the present greenery of the grasses and trees marks but a short interim between the ice ages for which the dales themselves long. It requires little imagination to feel the chill of winter here, even when the rough grasses and ferns are dancing in the sunlight.

A short drive or a longish walk across these dales takes us to the Buttertubs, which are the other natural wonder of this part of England.

The Buttertubs, a series of limestone stacks rising out of a labyrinth of deep pots, near the summit of Buttertubs Pass.

*Right: The free fall
of Hardraw Force,
which allows ample
room for people to
walk behind and
under the stream of
water.*

*Far right: Behind
one of the stacks of
the Buttertubs and
across a deep pot, a
stream can be seen
still eroding the
limestone, which
will ultimately
deepen the pot.*

Such a journey leads past many waterfalls, each
of which might well be regarded with awe in
any other context, but which may be passed
almost unnoticed by the traveller for whom
there is a surfeit of such beauties.

In the raised heart of the dales, yet by the side
of the road, are the Buttertubs themselves.
These are deep pots in the limestone, which can
be regarded as pronounced grykes, or as extensive clints, depending upon how you wish to
classify such freaks of nature. The water-worn
fissures have left tall 'stacks' towering upwards,
with their tops in most places still level with the
ground. When you look down at these white
limestone stacks, it is difficult to understand
why they have been called Buttertubs, for they
do not resemble butter tubs. It seems more
likely that they took their name from that for the
whole locality, the Buttertubs Pass. The first
part of the name perhaps came from the old
English *byden*, meaning 'valley', but the etymology is obscure.

The grykes (or pots, as they are sometimes
called) are very deep, ranging from fifty to a
hundred feet. In his fascinating book, *Journey
Through Britain*, John Hillsby records how at the
'Green Dragon' 'they will tell you that the holes
are bottomless, and, as one old man put it,
"some are deeper than that".' At times, however, you can peer into these pits and see, down
among the ferns and black dirt, the bodies or
bones of those unsuspecting sheep which have
ventured too close to these ravines for their own
good.

The word 'pot', used here, has nothing to do
with the word meaning 'drinking vessel', and in
fact comes from the Scandinavian word meaning 'deep hole' or 'abyss'. These pots are deeper
than the grykes of limestone pavements and are
formed not merely by acidic erosion but also by
the running water of streams. Such a stream can
be seen on the opposite page, still deepening
the pot-hole behind the limestone column.

There are actually two separate areas of deep

grykes, on either side of the road, although the casual visitor generally sees only the series to the right, coming from the direction of Hawes. The lesser-known series is to the left, about fifty yards further on.

When SPB Mais visited the Buttertubs, in preparation for a series of travelogues for the BBC, he saw them in the snow. He appears to have examined only the better-known series, which are signposted and which, in modern times at least, are approached by a safe concrete stepway. '... So we drove on over the top of the Butter Tubs, a weird series of limestone potholes by the side of the road. As I wandered over some apparently harmless, uneven, snow-covered humps of boulders and coarse grass, I found myself suddenly looking down a narrow, circular, limestone chasm or chimney, a crevasse that simply disappeared into the bowels of the earth, vertically. There are about a dozen of these in a dozen yards, and like the "forces" in the dales you don't see them till you're right on them.'

If the snow is deep, the chances are that you will not see the Buttertubs at all, and consequently care must be taken if you visit this pass in the wintertime. Even when the weather is good, the bones of sheep should serve as a reminder not to step too close to the edge of these labyrinthian pots.

The Cheesewring

The Cheesewring has all the appearance of
having been built by man. Despite studying
these stones from every angle and reading what
the geologists have to say about their formation
as eroded outcrops, it is still hard to believe that
the stones were not placed there deliberately.

The Cheesewring is a grey-blue balancing act
in granite. The largest of the capstones mea-
sures 34 feet in circumference, while those
below are only half that size. One has the
impression that a push from a human hand will
send them crashing into the quarry behind. In
his book, *The Stone Peninsula*, James Turner
ruminates on this possibility: 'A finger placed
on the right spot and the monument would
collapse. No one has yet found that spot in the
stones. They stand forever, gathering sun in
summer, in moorland exposure of wind and
weather which have moulded them into their
curious shapes.'

Curiously enough, despite its shape and size
and despite the fact that it is usually photographed from the slopes of Stowe's Hill, the
best view of the Cheesewring is from beyond
the far edge of the quarry. From this point you
see it balanced precariously on the quarry edge,
dwarfed somewhat by the gap, yet contrasting
as a vertical thrust against the horizontal stratifications of the quarry below.

This view is the grand finale to the finest walk
to the Cheesewring, which permits the contrast
of the slash of the quarry to develop against the
gentle undulations of the moorlands. The walk
starts at the edge of the village of Minions and
leads through the three ancient stone circles
called the 'Hurlers'. It is a fairly short distance,
but a long walk through history, for these
megalithic circles and their outliers are dated to
around 1500 BC. Recent excavations have revealed that the central circle of the three, which
is the largest, with a diameter of 135 feet, was
paved with granite slabs. A trackway with a
similar granite slab flooring leads from this
circle to the more northerly one.

*The stratified
erosion of the
Cheesewring,
balancing on its
insubstantial socle.*

23

The Cheesewring precariously situated at the edge of the quarry, as it is seen when approached over the moor by way of the Hurlers.

Nearer the Cheesewring and on the slopes of Stowe's Hill, there is an equally ancient burial barrow, which was somewhat incompetently excavated in the 1830s. These amateur digs revealed, among several skeletal remains, a number of artefacts and that most famous of all golden beakers, the Rillaton Cup. This is now displayed sedately in the British Museum, but in former times it was apparently used by William IV as a shaving mug!

As you saunter across this patch of history on Bodmin Moor, you find yourself gradually climbing the side of a hill, until you reach the unexpected chasm of the quarry and see across the gap the splendid Cheesewring. This quarry is not so vast as the more famous one at

Delabole on the north of Bodmin Moor, yet it is still large enough to accommodate St Paul's cathedral in London.

The Cheesewring itself bears an outlandish name. It is supposed to have been given to the stones because of their distinctive shape, which is said to resemble a cheese within the cloth, after the whey has been wrung out. However, these names rarely have such origins and, like others, it may well be a modern corruption of a much earlier name with a quite different meaning.

The stones are surrounded by a stone history – found not only in the quarry or in the ancient monuments scattered around the moor, but also in some buildings of more recent date. Nearby

One of the outliers of the northern circle of the Hurlers, contrasting with the Cornish 'castle' on the horizon.

is the 'house' of Daniel Gumb, a stonecutter who built himself this rude dwelling from rough blocks, and who is said to have raised a large family there. The single capstone on the front part of the house is carved with a simple diagram – perhaps intended to illustrate Pythagoras' theorem, or even containing some secret known only to Daniel Gumb. On a rock nearby he has carved his name and the date 1735. The name and date may have once stood on the house, too, but do no longer. Even the stones could hardly have protected the family he taught 'to brave solitude and cold in the cavern in the rocks as he braved them'. The quotation is from the writer Wilkie Collins, who told us the story a century later, and who may

unwittingly have foisted onto Cornish history what was merely a local joke.

All around, within sight of the Cheesewring and the Hurlers, are those other stone remains of a Cornish past which was bound up with the labour of mining. These are the 'castles', as they are somewhat romantically called – the pit-head remains which mark the shafts of the tin or copper mines. The miners themselves would hardly have thought of these monuments as 'castles': they marked for them a daily vertical climb up a thousand feet of rough ladders, out of the bowels of the earth, at the end of a long day of work. There is more romance in a single stone of the Cheesewring, than in all the stones of the many Cornish 'castles'.

Dover

The appeal of Dover ... is to the imaginations of men. The noble rampart of the chalk between Shakespeare's Cliff and the South Foreland bear, more perhaps than any other stretch of our coast, the burden of legendary England ...

Aubrey de Selincourt

From the sea the white cliffs of Dover are the symbolic gateways to England: the chalk precipices, though often reduced to grey in the rain-swept climate, are still defiant protectors of the island race. Yet from the land the white cliffs nowadays are elusive. They have been almost entirely covered, first by a facade of buildings, then by building improvements, and later by docks, dockland extensions and (final indignity) by a huge curving motorway which seemingly hangs before them in the skies and hides the cliff spectacular from the land. This is why it is best to see this most famous of English wonders from the sea: if you have to see it from the land, then do so from the cliff-walk, perhaps with your back to the rising sun.

Dover was built originally in a gorge, emerging from a meeting of two valleys, one of which runs down from Folkestone, the other from Canterbury. A long time ago, this meeting created a fine natural harbour: the very name 'Dover' points to the original reason for its existence, before it was choked first by nature and then by modern developments. The word Dover is from the archaic *dwr*, 'water' (which gave us also 'Door' – see Durdle Door), and this is why the river which still runs from the hidden mouth is called even now the Dour. In modern times the Dour is hidden as much as the cliffs themselves, for it is poured by conduits and tunnels into the sea, in order to leave room for the squares and buildings piled over the top.

The Dour estuary silted up with the passing of time, the result of that constant movement which is called by geologists the 'eastward drift'. The technical knowledge of earlier times simply could not cope with this drift: sand banks and hindering shingles would grow almost as rapidly as piers were built to deal with them. The most far-seeing of the enterprises to control and direct the eastward drift was made by the appropriately named Diggs, who dug an inner harbour, later called the Great Pent. This was designed to gather millions of gallons of seawater with each high tide, and then let it surge out to sweep away the detritus from the outer harbour. As is the way of things, this Great Pent was later 'improved' and then converted into the modern Wellington Dock.

The subsequent lines of improvements, such as the deepened docks, the floating docks, the piers and roads, gradually accumulated along the coast like so much silt. This had the effect of making this now quite unnatural harbour into a fine landing place for ships, ferries, hovercrafts and trains. The Channel Tunnel, or Channel Bridge, when it comes will be just another addition to this conglomeration called Dover, which has virtually committed suicide by being so close to Europe.

This proximity to the Continent has a tangled history. Just as the modern harbour is an accretion of structures in man's struggle against natural forces, so is Dover Castle an accretion in man's struggle against man. The site may originally have been an earth fort, but the visible remains indicate that the Romans built a light-house there (now said to be the oldest standing building in Britain) and perhaps also a large barracks. With the untidy withdrawal of military Rome, and the quiet arrival of Christian Rome, the site was turned into a monastery, making use of the old Roman walls. The immense castle was itself begun by William the Conqueror, intent on putting his seal to that audacious theft of England. 'The very key of England' is how the defiant Hugh de Burgh described Dover Castle in 1216 when he refused to yield it to a French Dauphin.

But to understand what impregnable Dover must have looked like in earlier times – to catch a glimpse of those cliffs which faced and deflected Julius Caesar – you can no longer look at Dover itself. You have to turn to the other magnificent cliffs to the east and west of Dover, all of which are of almost equal height, and in particular to the wonderful cliffs and beaches around St Margaret's Bay to the east, which are

The white cliffs above Dover, dwarfing yet enhancing the town. On the cliffs can be seen traces of battlements, built mainly during the Second World War against possible invasion.

virtually untouched and can easily evoke images of the past.

The cliffs to the west are called 'Shakespeare's Cliff' because of a famous scene in *King Lear*, described by blind Gloucester: 'There is a cliff, whose high and bending head looks fearfully in the confined deep.' It is here that Gloucester wishes to escape from the agony of his blinding by throwing himself over the edge, to fall on to the strand below, where 'The fishermen, that walk upon the beach, appear like mice'. Edgar, his son, who leads him here, and saves his life, constructs a mental picture of these high cliffs – 'the murmuring surge, that on th'unnumber'd pebbles chafes, cannot be heard so high. I'll look no more; lest my brain turn, and the deficient sight topple down headlong.'

It might reasonably be asked why Shakespeare should have chosen this area around Dover for his drama. Was it merely a matter of its being the site of the expected landing of the French armies in the play which led Gloucester to the place? I think that there is a hidden symbolism in the choice of this cliff for the 'suicide', since Dover is in Kent, and faces most nearly to the coasts of France. It was the Earl of Kent and the King of France who were the two supporters of King Lear, in whose championship Gloucester lost his eyes. The natural surroundings become a symbol of the forces raging around the King of England, and it is clear that in Shakespeare's day the cliffs were already a national image.

Right: The towering chalk cliffs west of St Margaret's Bay are less famous than the white cliffs of Dover further west, yet more impressive and unspoiled.

Flamborough Head

Danish words still linger in the local dialect, and a Danish king once sent envoys to Flamborough to record several words which had been forgotten in his country but were used in the village.

Edward Gower

In his pleasant and practical guide to Flamborough, Edward Gower likens the Head to a great whale. It would, of course, have to be a white-bellied whale with a green back of grass. The Anglo-Saxons had a less quaint image, for the name which they gave it, and which is still used today with a slightly changed sound, was *flaen*, meaning 'arrow point'. And, indeed, this jutting headland is much more like an arrow point than any whale.

Flamborough Head on the Yorkshire coast, has two faces. There is the angry or sullen face of winter, when the North Sea pounds and powders the grey cliffs, as though seeking to wrest them from the mainland; and there is the exquisitely serene aspect of snow-white cliffs, blue skies and the gentle lull of waves. Flamborough seems to wear either one or other of these two masks at all times, with no greys or half-lights between dark and sullen or bright and radiant.

In the early days, almost before the written history of England began, Flamborough Head was separated from the mainland by a huge man-made dyke. One or other of the pre-Roman tribes aided the sea in its struggle to make the headland an island, and cut a 2½-mile entrenchment from north to south, forming a promontory – a vast defended fort – of about ten square miles, perhaps the biggest cliff fort in the world. This Dane's Dyke can still be seen – 18 feet high in places – cutting from Cat Nab in the north, to Dane's Dyke Farm in the south. Those ancient labours are recalled in the name given to this part of England – Little Denmark. Because of the name some scholars argue that it was the Danes who made this immense fort, but on the other hand it might have been the fierce tribes of the Brigantes who cut the ditch and fortified the long ramparts – those very same Brigantes who almost managed to stem the might of Rome, two thousand years ago.

Historians record a quaint custom which obviously went back to the Danish occupation.

A sea-arch at the north landing of Flamborough Head. This bulbous peninsula is only joined to the mainland by a narrow land-bridge, and one day will detach to form an islet or stack.

31

Each year, in the time of Henry VIII, the head of the local Constable family would call over to Denmark from the cliff edge to tell the Danes that if they wanted their levy then he would give it to them. When there was no answering response from the Danish mainland, he would fix a coin to an arrow and fire it across the waves. It is said that this *Danegelt* was a rent paid to the ancient Danish landowners.

Flamborough Head is also rich in caves, coves and promontories, and, as is general with such places, it became the favoured resort of smugglers. The white cliffs are welcoming from the landward side, but a terrible challenge from the seas. The arrow-shaped northern landing is the most interesting perhaps, since it has natural

Above: A sea-arch in the eroded cliffs to the north of the headland pictured on the previous page.

inlets on either side. The cliffs towards the south landing do not tower quite so proudly, the two-hundred-foot chalk battlements sink down to rest and and caves no longer proliferate. The caves which infest the headland have curious names – Breil Cave, St George's Hole, the Common Hole, the Dovecote, the Kirk Hole and Smuggler's Cave. The latter is especially beautiful, with its white marble picked out in veins of rich colour, but the real wonder of Flamborough lies not in its caves, nor its modest height, but in the sheer accumulation of small bays and precipitous cliffs, marked by a not too patient sea, which polishes the cliffs to dazzle the eyes on a clear sunlit day.

The walk across the tip of headland from the north landing towards the lighthouse is perhaps the most beautiful walk in Yorkshire. Even on a gentle day the wind presses itself into the walking body, and increases the dizziness as the two hundred feet of chalk tumble to the sea. The appearance of the lighthouse which rewards this walk is in itself quite unremarkable, until one learns that this 90-foot structure was built in 1806 by a local man without the use of scaffolding, and that he completed it in less than a year – some say in five months.

Near the lighthouse a bronze plaque commemorates a battle between British and American ships just off the headland in 1779. The *Bonhomme Richard*, leading ship of the American squadron and sporting for the first time in European waters the 'Stars and Stripes', was commanded by the colourful John Paul Jones, 'the father of the US Navy'. He was originally a Scotsman from Kirkcudbrightshire and in this 'bloody engagement' off Flamborough Head on 23 September he is reported to have captured two British men-of-war – not, in fact, his first victory against the English. John Paul Jones was known as the Pirate with some justification, for at one time he was mate of a slaver. He emerged into respectable history as a commander at the time of America's first naval success, capturing the English ship *Drake* in Belfast Lough.

Another unusual aspect of this place is its geographical position, for Land's End is 362 miles to the south-west, while John O'Groats is 362 miles north. The north/south orientation of the Head is unexpected, for one certainly has the impression that one is looking east when facing the sea. However, it is possible to stand on the headland and watch the blood-red majesty of the sunset in what one expects to be the north. It is as though the cutting of that ancient Dyke did, indeed, sever the headland and permit it to twist round so that it could face back towards Denmark.

Above: The southernmost of the peninsulas frames the north landings and is infested with caves and stacks. In this stretch of cliffs is the famous Smuggler's Cave.

Gordale Scar

One of the most awe-inspiring wonders in the country.

Arthur Gaunt

Gordale Scar is neighbour to Malham Cove, and there is a natural tendency to compare the two wonders of the Yorkshire Dales, and even to debate which is the more remarkable, although, as formations, they are very different.

Malham Cove declares itself from a distance: the majestic stretch of its amphitheatre is visible from almost a mile across the valley, and its immense scale is grasped immediately. Gordale Scar, on the other hand, reveals its wonders slowly: after a half-mile walk along the beautiful valley of Gordale Beck, you come to a tall fissure in the cliffs, and only then, when hemmed in by the overhanging rocks which tower four hundred feet above, do you begin to form a picture of how vast this chasm really is.

The dark walls narrow into a small rough and boulder-strewn enclave, backed by a wall of rocks and waterfalls which must be climbed if further progress is to be made. This climb leads into a further raised valley, itself strewn with boulders and coursed by a rapid stream. Off up to the right of this valley there are descending waterfalls (one of them spouting through a porthole opening of a natural arch) which feed the streams and rivulets. Behind is the sheer-walled chasm cut out of the rock by earth faults and the persistence of water. If there are people in this lower valley, they appear from this vantage point like pinheads within the dark belly of the chasm.

The roar of water above and the breath-taking chasm below form a total contrast with the glinting limestone of Malham, yet the Scar is just as much a product of the Craven Fault as is the Cove. The Scar was very probably a vast underground cavern before the last Ice Age. The roof collapsed leaving the vertical walls and filling the floor with debris. The rock fall was then partly washed away by the river and water streams.

The waterfalls of the Scar are especially impressive when the rains have been heavy. At such times, however, it is the higher falls which

must be seen for the true wonder of the place to be appreciated. A climb up the rocks during full spate is by no means for the faint-hearted, since the echo of tumbling water is magnified by natural acoustics to an almost frightening pitch, and the sheer walls of dark limestone seem about to crash down.

As late as 1730 a thunderstorm did change the upper structure of the cliffs. Until then there had been a lake in the headland cavities above, and the water from this lake poured over the cliff edge near the centre of the chasm. The pressure of water during the thunderstorm breached the upper walls allowing all the water to discharge through the side of the gorge. The lake was lost, but a new and spectacular water-fall was created from the old lake-feed.

Anyone who is agile enough to climb up to the spout above will observe a most interesting phenomenon. There is no doubt that the upper falls are more savage and wild than the lower ones: more water pours into the gorge than can be seen running out of it in the relatively gentle Gordale Beck. Here we have, in fact, an ex-ample of history repeating itself, for some of the water discharged from Malham Tarn, which flows through the natural arch, finds its way underground. This means that another deep cave system is being carved below the floor of the Scar; no doubt the day will come when there will be another collapse of a cave roof, to leave an even deeper gorge at Gordale.

Far left: The chasm of Gordale, seen from above the first of the waterfalls.

Above: A view from the porthole through which pours the main waterfall that feeds Gordale. The diminutive human figure gives some idea of the massive scale of the Scar.

Right: The porthole with the main waterfall of Gordale, seen from the rocky plateau above the lower falls. This stream of water does not find its way completely into the rift below – some of it is lost underground and is presumably carving another cave system.

Below: The view into the Scar from the entrance. The Cliffs tower on either side, and a waterfall pours over a blockage of rocks which can be scaled to reach a raised plateau.

Above: The chasm of Gordale seen from above the display of waters. From this vantage point one can see how the Scar was formed when the roof of an immense cave fell in.

Gordale Scar is a desolate place, carrying with it something of the sense of tragedy and loneliness which appealed to the English Romantic poets. The popular notion that the name 'Gordale' has a connection with the word 'gore' may arise from this horrifying desolation, or perhaps even from the legends (which also abound in many other places far from Gordale) of the lovers who chose to leap from the cliff top rather than be separated. In fact, the name Gordale is derived from the Scandinavian term, *geir*, which meant 'an angular shape' and which is still a term used in dress-making. This ancient word is joined with the Scandinavian *dalr*, 'parcel of land', the two combining to give us a perfect description of its shape.

36

'This precipice, so lofty and so sheer ... seems to have possessed a singular faculty of terrifying poets', as Arthur Norway remarks in his *Highways and Byways in Yorkshire*. Wordsworth gave us a sonnet on Gordale, but the sonnet he wrote at Gordale is merely sad. He pictures the Gordale chasm as a lair for young lions and as the abode of a water-god, but here one feels no need to transport lions to cold Yorkshire or to conjure local deities, in order to intensify the sense of awe about the place. Thomas Gray was more honest and personal when he commented on his visit which took place long before that of Wordsworth: 'I stayed there not without shuddering for a quarter of an hour, and thought my trouble richly repaid for the impression which will last with life.'

A vast and romantic vision of Gordale may still be seen in the Tate Gallery, London. John Ward painted an immense canvas about three years before Wordsworth wrote the unfortunate sonnet, showing us a wilder Gordale than may be seen today, as though the years of tourism have tamed the place. Among the rocks and falls are fighting stags, a powerful white bull and a herd of cattle – not a single one of which will be found here in modern times. It must be remembered, however, that Ward painted this picture for Lord Ribblesdale, and the artist was probably more concerned with capturing the appearance of the Lord's rare herd of wild white beasts than with the structure of the Scar itself.

Perhaps Ward's view of the Scar carries us just a little nearer to its ice-age origin, for in those days animals of a very different breed frequented the place. West of nearby Malham is Victoria Cave, where the bones of the woolly rhinoceros, the mammoth, bear and arctic fox have been found, all evocative of a very different Malham to the one we know today. One wonders what strange animals perished when the roof of this great cavern collapsed, many thousands of years ago.

37

Henhole

From . . . the Henhole is one of the more dramatic ascents of the Cheviot . . .

John Philipson

Henhole, the rock- and scree-strewn chasm leading into the Cheviot Hills – wild, savage and drear, even in the sunshine.

The rolling Cheviot Hills are now clothed in gentle greens, and in parts are shaded by peaceful forests, but beneath the tamed surface lies the evidence of a violent past. Under the soft fern roots and springing turf are the rocks and hardened lava flows of mighty volcanoes which dominated this part of England, and gave it its present shape. When the wild volcanic display cooled off, it left thrusts of grey granite dykes, granite ridges and soft smoothed hills, which over the millennia have been eroded, forming hard ravines in the soft grazing lands of the Cheviots. Bare crags fold into the valleys, which are littered with the fall of scree and boulders, but the fast-flowing streams carry away the pebbles and smaller stones, diverting themselves around the larger boulders.

Most wonderful of these carved ravines and valleys are those called the Bizzle and the Henhole. The latter especially is a magnificent and solitary display of wild waterfalls, enclosed by scree-strewn granite cliffs, where apart from wild animals only seasoned walkers and climbers go.

The Henhole cuts deeply into the western side of the green Cheviots, an unexpected chasm in the granite. Its boulder-strewn floor is negotiated by a fast-flowing stream, which with its exquisite movement of waterfalls and cascades contrasts powerfully with the static quality of the dark cliffs and produces an element of joy almost out of place in this dour valley. None of the waterfalls is very high – three or four of them are little over eighteen feet – and they are pigmies in comparison to the nearby Linhope Spout in the Breamish valley, which tumbles its water down another lava dyke wall. But their very number and their diversity of forms, colours and music make the long haul up College Valley to the Henhole worth the trip. Indeed, it is the variety and delight of these cascades which make the Henhole a natural wonder.

The curious word, 'Henhole', is not a polite

Above: The soft green undulations of the Cheviots, cut by ancient stream-flows. This view was taken from the hillside of College Valley, and looks over towards the Cheviots above the Henhole.

one in the north of England where it can mean a dirty, unpleasant place. Almost certainly the name is a corruption derived from the Middle English *heng*, meaning 'hanging' – a word which is found also in the name Stonehenge. Probably the *Henghole* was descriptive of the small cave, now called Cannon Hole, which 'hangs' high up in the grey granite facing of this valley. This granite face, with its hole of a cave, is well known to climbers, and several climbs have been charted in detail up these dark crags. A difficult one is that named Black Adam's Corner, but the one that calls for the greatest expertise is the Cannon Hole Direct, an almost vertical climb of 120 feet up one side of this ancient weathered chasm in the Cheviot Hills.

Since mediaeval times the rock outcrop on the Pennine Way leading to the Henhole has similarly been called the 'Hanging Stone'. Such outcrops – and the cliffs, depressions and screes of the Henhole – are like so many dark bones breaking through the soft surface of the Cheviots. These hills are now delicate undulations of green hues, but in far distant times the original landscape was that of tangled woodlands. An idea of this can be gained from the countryside near Lambden Burn, where the bottom of College Valley still nurses its trees from the hills.

*Left: One of the
many waterfalls
which tumble
through the valley
of the Henhole.
This fall is perhaps
sixteen or seventeen
feet high; what the
falls lack in stature,
they gain in variety
and delight, being
the only element of
life and movement
in this dark valley.*

High Force

Of the fall itself there is often nothing to be seen except a great curtain of spray rising out of the ravine eighty feet into the air and drenching every-thing in a fine mist, often with a rainbow on its fringe ... You feel like shouting with the exhilaration of it all.

Harry J Scott

High Force announces itself gently to the ears as you approach along public footpaths through the splendid woodland scenery of Teesdale. Rocks and thick trees with delicately coloured roots and leaves hive off the full noise until the very last moment. Then, when you turn the corner to face the head of the Tees valley, you stand as if transfixed by the cacophony and wetted by the far-flung spume from the cauldron which receives the boiling waters of the force.

The falls are no mere display of white water against dark granite – a contrast which would no doubt have its own beauty. They in fact present a more dramatic picture of white spume and red-brown waters which boil against a background of dark rock. The contrast of hues is caused by the peat which colours the swollen waters and produces almost a stained-glass effect within the falls.

High Force is oddly named, for it is by no means one of the highest waterfalls in England. Even the nearby Cauldron Snout, a few miles up the River Tees, is higher (although it is really a series of cataracts). High Force plunges some seventy feet over a series of cyclopean granite steps but it has all the appearance of being one single fall as monumental as anything you will

High Force in full spate, with a rainbow in the early morning sunlight playing around its feet.

find in Britain. Perhaps the name – probably derived from the same Nordic roots as Hoy – is used to distinguish it from Low Force, further along the Tees, between Bowlees and Winch Bridge. The word 'force' is still in common usage as a term for waterfall in the north, and has its roots in the Scandinavian tongue.

Without doubt, the best time to visit High Force is after a long period of rain, when the might of the swollen falls is such that even the distant viewing platform is not free of the wind-carried water. At these times it is difficult to take photographs because of the rapidity with which the camera lens is covered by fine spray. On the other hand, the spray can create some quite magical effects for the eyes. Since the river runs

from west to east, an early morning visit will at times give the spectator the opportunity to see one of the falls with a rainbow playing around its feet.

These are savage falls of water, even when seen from the platform beyond the cauldron, but they are almost unbelievable from the top of the precipice, for from here the eye is swept pell-mell by the swollen brown waters into the valley below. Guidebooks talk of the River Tees above the cataracts as a contrast to the fury below – 'little more than a burn bumbling along over the rocks' says Edward Grierson, for example – but one can only assume that such writers have never climbed up there when the Tees is in full flood. At such times, nothing

above these cyclopean rocks is safe.

When only one of the cataracts is seething with activity, it is possible, with some agility, to walk across the top of the northern fork of the Tees and onto the rock spur, from which point you can peer down on the boiling waters below. But this is only possible when High Force is not at its best, for then the display is too savage for a crossing, and the cauldron below resounds to the full orchestration of water-made sound, trapping the rainbows in its streaming sheets of spume.

Even without the romantic wildness of High Force, this valley which has been carved from the granite by Tees water would be worth a visit. The path towards the falls winds through some of the most beautiful woodland and rocks, yet the climax of the walk – seeing the tumbling waters of the Tees – makes this no mere ramble through nature, more a pilgrimage of wonder.

In his book, *Modern Painters*, Ruskin referred especially to these falls in order to describe how water drops differently under different situations. With a particular watercolour by Turner in mind, he wrote: 'Thus in the Upper Fall of the Tees, though the whole basin of the fall is blue and dim with the rising vapour, yet the whole attention of the spectator is directed to that which it was peculiarly difficult to render, the concentric zones and delicate curves of the falling water itself; and it is impossible to express with what exquisite accuracy these are

Tree roots, exposed rocks and wild flowers proliferate in the wild valley which borders the edge of the rocky chasm of the Tees to the east of High Force. This valley lies along the route from the main road to the falls.

given . . . Now water will leap a little way, and it will leap down a weir or over a stone, but it *tumbles* over a high fall like this . . . when we have lost the *spring* of the fall, and arrived at the *plunge* of it, then we begin really to feel its weight and wildness . . . it is then that it begins to writhe, and twist, and sweep out zone after zone in wilder stretching as it falls, and to send down the rocket-like lance-pointed, whizzing shafts at its sides, sounding for the bottom.' I sympathize with Ruskin, for the majesty of High Force does tend to evoke purple passages in the mind of the spectator. Indeed, I am surprised that Ruskin, who wrote so observantly on all natural forms, did not make more reference to this exquisite river garden.

Land's End

In summer the Land's End is no land at all, its incense is the smell of fish and chips ... In summer the Land's End is nothing. It waits only for winter and the great seas ...

James Turner

The most westerly cliffs of England – Land's End – stretch into the Atlantic towards the inundated land known to the ancients and now surviving only in myth and folklore.

The granite cliff face of the most westerly point of Land's End is also land's beginning, and it is almost possible to imagine that on a clear day you can see across those seven hundred miles to John O'Groats. Here, England has been channelled down as though into a bottleneck, first through narrowing Devon, then into the garden of Cornwall, until suddenly there is land no more, and only the sound of the waves, the sight of a few rocks and sea. Beyond is the sea-beleaguered lighthouse of the Longships, a speck two miles to the west and reaching some 123 feet above the sea, although at times the waves are so high that they lash against the top of the lantern.

The cliffs along this coast are high – between Portreath and Land's End, for example, those at Hell's Mouth are a vertical 200 feet, but the height decreases as they push out last westward fingers, and the final rocks are sometimes only 60 feet above the waves.

This is more than a natural wonder, of course; it is a national institution, so that on all but the very bleakest day you will not stand here alone. Tourists swarm to this end of our land, as though anxious to be free of its small compass. They peer over the drop, down into those savage breakers which still erode the foundations of Cornwall, and after a moment or so they turn away towards the cafes and the shops, to a more familiar warmth.

The true voyager, however, does not turn away quite so quickly to that other world, and is content to look out into the dreaming seas. Beyond these reaches of sea there once was found the fabled country of Atlantis – the lost land which gave that sea its name. But even nearer at hand, there was another Cornish Atlantis which appears in later histories – even in the Anglo-Saxon Chronicles. This is the stretch of sea-covered land between the granite cliffs of this westerly point and the Scillies, a land which is now marked only by the rocks which make the area almost unnavigable. It is

Above: One of the sea-arches to the east of Land's End. The whole of this line of cliffs is a wonderland of eroded forms.

Far right, above: The cliff face below Land's End.

Far right, below: The weathered, lichen-covered boulders on top of the headland.

said that this was the ancient country of 'Lyonesse', a fertile land owned and tilled by a wonderful people; it is said also, as in many such inundated lands, that bells from submerged churches can still be heard. Cornish fishermen have reported such submarine tolling, and have insisted that the roofs of houses can still be seen at low tide.

In the exquisite prose of *The Stone Peninsula*, James Turner laments the loss of Lyonesse, but also prays that it be kept away from the prying eyes of men. Far better to let Lyonesse remain in the minds of the romantic dreamers. 'And although I have not been so lucky myself I know people who have stood on Cape Cornwall and, looking westward, have seen that city of Lyonesse, or its mirage, rise again from the sea as it was in 1099. They speak of marble bright with light and the peculiar green of the houses.'

Returning to the present and still ignoring the tourist cafes and the road behind, one can take a pathway to the left which follows a fascinating

route through an undulating wilderness of coastlines. The five or six miles' walk to the Logan Rock can be extended almost indefinitely in space and time for anyone who is inclined to labour along the magnificent ups and downs which the cliffs and coves provide.

At Land's End – and also in a tunnel under Land's End – the two seas, the Atlantic and the English Channel, crash together, continuing their fight out over a raggle of rocks in the direction of the Scilly Isles; the name brings to mind the eels that are still caught there, since they were once called *sillys*.

Yet, even with all the wildness of the scene, and all the power of nature, it is certain that Land's End owes its fame to its siting rather than to its beauty. There are cliffs within a few miles' walk which are more impressive, more rugged and beautiful, but there is certainly something remarkable about the bluestone granite which faces so bravely the almost constant lash of the Atlantic waves.

Ruskin, in support of his genius, Turner, painted a savage word picture of Land's End, portraying the waves of the Atlantic as an army defeated by the stalwart armies of rocks, 'throwing all behind it into disorder, breaking up the succeeding waves into vertical ridges, which in their turn, yet more totally scattered upon the shore, retire in more hopeless confusion, until the whole surface of the sea becomes one dizzy whirl of rushing, writhing, tortured, undirected rage, bound and crashing, and coiling in an anarchy of enormous power . . .' Words cannot express more fully this elemental anarchy.

There is rarely a full calm day around these rocks, as though the sea was anxious to swallow Cornwall with the same ease that she long ago swallowed the fabled Atlantis. On a full storm day it is easy to believe this will happen, for the waves explode like shells against the granite, and the water tries to justify the ancient Cornish name for this peninsula, the Pednan-Laaz, 'the end of the earth'.

Lindisfarne

'I want to catch the 5.39 at Beal,' I said.
'And what time might that be?' he asked.
How glorious to live on an island where time
matters as little as that.

S P B Mais

Right: The richly pebbled strand of Lindisfarne, looking directly south from below the volcanic extrusion of the Beblowe.

Far right: The castle on the Beblowe just before sunset, with the mainland behind.

To describe Holy Island as magical seems fatuous, for almost every writer so describes it, yet no other word will quite do. It is too open an island to be mysterious, yet it is steeped in a special atmosphere, as though bathed in an aura from its past, when it was the cradle of Christianity in these lands. It is indeed a *holy* island still, and dreams mingle with reality in this place. It is not surprising to learn that the vertebrae of prehistoric fish, which are hunted on the beaches to make necklaces, are called 'St Cuthbert's beads'. I am not sure which is more remarkable, that ancient fish bones should be hung around modern necks, or that an ancient saint should be remembered in modern times, in an unconscious symbolism of the early Church which linked the fish with Christ. Time is curiously displaced on this powerful island, on an even deeper level than that recorded (above) by Mais on his trip to Lindisfarne, for the visible and tangible world seems to slip away. I suppose that I must admit myself defeated, and describe the island, like all the others, as being quite magical.

The lovely and appropriate name, 'Holy Island', was first used in the eleventh century, while the names 'Lindisfarne' and 'Farne' (for the dark islands to the north) are very ancient. It is essentially a volcanic sill, a minor eruption of the lower magmas in the earth, now hardened, and still being moulded by the seas. The most distinctive feature of the island is, of course, the huge volcanic protuberance once called the Beblowe, which is said by the more imaginative to have been thrown here from the eruption of the Cheviot volcano, but which, a geologist assures me, had its own subterranean fire and pressure. A volcanic extrusion of basalt, Lindisfarne is the land termination of the Great Whin Sill, a series of jagged ridges of dark rock running across Northumberland, which pierce the light limestone base. The name 'island' is not altogether fair, for only at times is it a true island across the tidal flats. Often, the approach

from Beal proves disappointing on a first visit, since its distinctive form, the volcanic castle-topped intrusion, is not visible and, where one expects sea, there are mud flats. The man-made causeway which carries traffic across to the island is about three miles long: only the first part is across the sand flats, and just over two miles of it curves around the southern parts to the priory which gave Lindisfarne its later name.

In mediaeval times, when the activity and influence of the priory was at its height, the tidal stretch was negotiated by means of the stepping stones which are still clearly marked by posts to the south of the present causeway. This gives the actual direction of the original pilgrim's way. It was here that 'Twice every day the waves efface of staves and sandalled feet the trace', as Walter Scott put it in his *Marmion*. The crossing was very different for those early

pilgrims to St Aidan's Priory, for it followed the full three-mile circuit, and had its own refuge towers against the tides, and a crossing certainly involved a drenching from the tide streams, even when the waters were low.

The growth of Christianity in Northumberland actually began with Edwin, King of Northumbria, who was the first Christian king, but he was defeated in 633. The whole of Northumbria was devastated and lapsed into paganism. His nephew Oswald soon gained the throne, and fortunately for Christianity he had received his education in Iona: this was sufficient for him to invite his old teachers to send him a bishop for the area. This request eventually brought in no less a person than St Aidan, who chose for his seat not the expected places of York or Durham but the island of Lindisfarne. The religion thrived and brought much fame to the island.

There are hints of the stark piety of the times

The distinctive Beblowe, topped by the castle, gives the otherwise flat island its characteristic form. Here, it is viewed from the small village to the west.

in the work of the Venerable Bede, who tells of St Cuthbert's passion for the coast of Northumberland. Despite this love of the coast the ascetic saint dug himself a cell-pit which had a view only of the skies, so as not to be distracted by all this wild beauty, 'that he might be wholly bent on heavenly things ... might behold nothing but the heavens above him'. There are touching stories, also, of sea otters who came to him from the waves as he prayed, and tried to warm his cold feet with their breath.

When St Cuthbert died in 687, he was buried, as he had requested, in Lindisfarne. The monks who, eleven years later, decided to move his body, found it still whole and incorrupt. It was placed in an oaken coffin, carved with the shapes of beasts, flowers and various images, and carried by the monks during enforced retreats from Viking raids. Fragments of the coffin are now in Durham Cathedral Museum but legend has it that the body of St Cuthbert was removed soon after the destruction of the monasteries by the Vikings, and its whereabouts is known only to the Benedictines.

The Lindisfarne Gospels constitute one of the most beautiful manuscripts in the world. It was penned by the monks of this tranquil island only a few years after the death of Cuthbert, towards the end of the seventh century, and includes a delightful, doubtless autobiographical, postscript, added as a later colophon: 'And Alfred, an unworthy and most miserable

the eighth century the first of the Vikings appeared, the monastery was devastated and most of its inhabitants were murdered. A fresh wave of Danish invasion in 873 drove the monks away, on their long pilgrimage with the monastic treasures, relics, the famous Gospels, and St Cuthbert's coffin.

A new monastery was founded by monks from Durham on Lindisfarne, in 1082, and it was from about this time that the island received its name 'Holy'. It is the remains of the eleventh-century buildings (with later additions, mainly up to the fourteenth century) which are still on the island, virtually everything of the earlier period having been lost. The adjacent St Mary's Church is something of a disappointment after the restoration of 1860, but the interior is of the same date as the monastery. Lindisfarne Castle, even though it bears the older name, is much later than the religious buildings, its stone being filched from the monastery after the dissolution ordered by Henry VIII. This castle resisted a siege by Parliamentarians, was captured in the Jacobite Rebellion of 1715, and then suffered at the hands of the nineteenth-century restorers.

The island which men call 'Holy' remains today as a serene and unaffecting background to all these matters of history.

The mud-flats of Lindisfarne at low tide, when passage to the island is possible by road. This view (with the mainland in the distance) shows the area formerly crossed by pilgrims on foot.

priest, with God's help and St Cuthbert's over-glossed it in English'. This manuscript was supposed to have been miraculously washed ashore after being lost in a storm off Ireland, during the monks' seven years of weary wanderings, carrying the coffin of their saint.

The Council of Whitby, called in 664 by the King of Northumbria, was effectively to put an end to the real power of Lindisfarne, for it led to the adoption of the rituals of the Roman Church, rather than those of the Celtic Church which had been established in such monastic settlements in earlier times.

The peace of Lindisfarne, which spread through the whole of Britain, did not last for much more than a century, for before the end of

The Logan Stone

Tradition said a giant had put it there and only a giant could push it over.

John Hillaby

The rocky coastline which stretches from Penzance to Land's End is finally reduced and swept clean at the sand beach of Porthcurno, as if the Atlantic breakers needed a rest from their Herculean task of sculpting rock. To the east of this beach, but nestled into the wild and rocky scenery, is the magnificent promontory upon which is delicately lodged one of the most famous stones of Cornwall – the Logan Stone.

This is a granite rock weighing sixty or more tons. Although guidebooks say that a touch will set it in motion ('poised so delicately that a touch can set it rocking', as a guide published in 1967 put it) this does not appear to be quite true. I have personally scaled the cliffs upon which this rock is balanced, and I have heaved with all my strength at the block, but all to no avail. The rock would not budge. No doubt a suitable lever could make the stone sway, but it can hardly be called a rocking stone. Yet, certainly, at one time it was a rocking stone. A famous story told about it gives proof of this. Aside from the wild beauty of the place, and the ancient rock fort of Treen Dinas (of the first century BC), it is this which attracts and entertains the visitors to this rough peninsula.

Lieutenant Goldsmith, the nephew of the famous poet Oliver, was commander of a cutter which frequently sailed the seas along this dangerous stretch of Cornish coast. For some reason which is not entirely clear (perhaps he was drunk), the Lieutenant decided to make the Logan Stone rock its last. Accordingly, one day in 1824, he landed a boat's crew alongside the rocks of the peninsula, and then with the aid of spikes and men he had the stone dislodged, so that it crashed to the earth below.

The action was sufficient to enrage the locals, as well as certain august personalities within the Admiralty, so the cumbersome bureaucratic machinery of the sea-lords creaked into action. Eventually the Lieutenant was commanded to replace the fallen stone – which, of course, proved a harder job than the dislodging. It took

several months and a total cost of £124 10s.6d., a sum which in those days would have been sufficient to build several houses. The end of the tale usually has it that the Lieutenant was financially ruined by this venture, but this is not the case. The end of the story is a little more sad than the ruin of one man, for, as Arthur Mee records in his *Cornwall*, the stone never rocked again with its former ease, and as a result the nearby village of Treen was itself almost ruined: 'It is said to have lost so much custom from visitors after the stone's fall that it came to be called Lieutenant Goldsmith's Deserted Village.'

The word *dinas* meant 'fort', and so it is not surprising that this headland of Treen Dinas

The rocky peninsula of Treen Dinas is a repository of ancient forts and of the Logan Stone.

should be the site of extensive earthworks and stone fortifications, mainly of Iron Age construction. The most southern of these, a bank faced with heavy masonry, with a central entrance, must be climbed if one wishes to reach the Logan Stone, which stands across a narrow gap to the south. It is likely that this inner rampart, being higher than the outlying works, was built in order to provide a better position from which to fire slingstones at any invaders advancing inland.

In the finest weather which Cornwall can produce, the Logan Stone is romantic enough, but in mist the stone and its setting are deeply mysterious, the conjurer of poetic images in the mind of the beholder.

The Logan Stone, which rocks no more, is here seen from across the natural trench which separates it from the ancient man-made wall of a defensive fort.

Right: The ravine of Lydford Gorge is covered in thick undergrowth, and was once the stronghold of robbers and cut-throats.

Far right: The lower part of the ravine of Lydford Gorge is approached from the bottom along a concrete path and then specially hung planks, from which one can peer into the swirling waters of the Devil's Cauldron.

Lydford Gorge

There are no kingfishers on Sundays in Lydford Gorge ... It is such a well-known beauty spot that these sensitive birds keep out of the way when there are too many people about, but for the rest of the week you may see them there, and herons too.

Sir Darrell Bates

Lydford Gorge is a vast gash in the earth, a mile and a half in length, with steep ravine walls which in places are over sixty feet high. It looks as though a giant struck at the edge of Dartmoor with an axe, leaving a fissure which sucked in a river and slowly filled with trees.

But it was no giant of mythology which wrenched this gorge into the earth; it was a giant of nature. Nearly half a million years ago the shifting of the ices diverted the river Lyd into a stream bed which was eroded by the swift waters; over the ages which followed, the river gouged a ravine into the landscape. To this day one can see all the outward signs of the ice movement in the trapped boulders, the pot-holes and glass-smooth basins, and also feel the ancient savagery in the atmosphere of this strangely elemental place.

Despite its cruel shaping through history, the ravine has its gentle parts. To the untrained eye, at least, the hues of the flowers, the wild garlic (the pervasive scent of which floats at times through the whole valley) and the languid trout in the river pools offer little sign of the incredible cataclysms of nature which formed this cleft.

In the dark, wild pockets we need no fantasy to help us imagine that this was once the home of those terrible outlaws under the command of the 'King of the Gubbings', who found fame in Kingsley's *Westward Ho!* 'Their wealth consisteth of other men's goods; they live by stealing the sheep on the moors ... Such is their fleetness, they will outrun many horses; vivaciousness, they outlive most men; living in an ignorance of luxury, the extinguisher of life. They hold together like bees; offend one, and all will revenge his quarrel.' It was on the edge of this gorge, also, that the early 'castle' of Lydford was built by the Normans, as a prison. It was used infamously as a prison by the tin-miners who ruled Dartmoor in later days – the 'most heinous, contagious and detestable place in the realm', in the words of an official description

The White Lady falls at the western end of the gorge. The lower half is not really a fall, as the water streams over almost vertical rocks.

published in 1512. Behind the prison and just beyond the nearby church are Iron Age earthworks, now overgrown by Eastern Cleave Wood. This wood runs into the deep and gloomy escarpment which shields Devil's Cauldron, and under the bridge which gave Lydford its name.

The part of Lydford Gorge which chills the soul in modern times and speaks openly of the wrecking force of nature is towards the eastern end of the gorge. Here the Devil's Cauldron lies deep in a cleft beneath the road bridge. It is approached at first by way of steps and bridges, then by paths cut into the side of a dark crevice, and finally, with some difficulty, across chainheld planks. This deep cauldron, with its boiling cataract and black rocks, is aptly named. The dark savagery of the place is reminiscent of its near namesake at Devil's Bridge, in Wales.

At the other extreme of the gorge – the western end – is a more delicate wonder, in beauty and gracious form the opposite of the turbulent darkness of the Cauldron. This is the White Lady waterfall, which has all the appearance of free fall some hundred feet in depth. In fact, the waters do not drop unbroken, since for half the height of fall they stream down the topmost rocks.

In between the black Cauldron and this white water there is a profusion of undergrowth and bushes, edging around the river Lyd and screened in by tree-infested slopes and cliffs. In the higher extremes of the gorge, the roots and branches have struggled to keep a foothold, and the rich intertwinings of their forms have produced a kind of fairy-tale world, which that great fairy-painter, Arthur Rackham, would have peopled with gnomes, elves or sylphs. One is unlikely ever to *see* these supernatural beings, and it could be, as Sir Darrel Bates insists, that kingfishers cannot be seen in the gorge on Sundays. But certainly it is possible to see them there on other days, along with the herons stalking their fishy prey in the Lyd. Spotted woodpeckers, too, can be seen burying their beaks in the oaks.

The finely balanced contrasts of this gorge almost suggest preternatural planning. One end encloses a savage turbulence, a wild, whirling crevice of darkness, a slit of black space savagely sliced into the rock, while the other opens out a shimmer of white translucence, a free-playing display of clear light from the rocks above. Darkness fighting the light, the very stuff of epic tales, and the two extremes which the German poet Goethe so rightly said lay at the root of all phenomena.

The trees which precariously grip the sides of the gorge are especially beautiful because of the richness of their root formations. This is caused by rapid soil erosion in the steep ravine.

Malham Cove

What we most enjoy in the Dales today is there because of what happened to this part of the earth a million or more years ago.

Harry J Scott

Snow lends a powerful intensity to the panorama of Malham Cove. To the right, behind the large boulder, is the rift along which flows the stream from the bottom of the Cove.

Malham Cove, that 'awful cliff filling up the valley with a sheer cross wall, and from beneath a black lip at the foot', as Charles Kingsley described it, is a magnificent natural amphitheatre, a dramatic fragment of the mid-Craven fault which runs across Ingleton. It is a massive, white stratification of limestone facing set amidst the natural greenery of the Yorkshire moors, some three hundred feet high, and three hundred yards across.

This white slash of limestone is so vast that it is best studied from a distance. The finest panorama is had from the side of Cove Road: from a closer position the immensity overwhelms one, and something of the wonder is lost, for it can be seen as just another cliff face, with a tiny beck bubbling from its base, instead of the gigantic ancient sculpture which it is.

Clearly, in the distant past, this arc of limestone must have been the site of an immense waterfall. During the last Ice Age the limestone grykes or fissures at the top would have sealed up with hard ice, and the waters from the melted snows would have streamed over the Cove in a splendid display – it might well have been the most magnificent waterfall in Britain. Now the limestone-strewn valley above the Cove is merely called 'Dry Valley', which, some say, is the covering of an immense cavern possibly as large as that which formed Gordale Scar.

The dark vertical patches on these white strata are formed by lichen and moss growths, encouraged by water seepage down through the limestone. These gave the original idea for Charles Kingsley's *The Water Babies*. It seems that in jest Kingsley explained these dark markings by saying they might as well have been made by a chimney sweep falling over the cliff edge, and sliding down the face. No wonder that the little hero of this wonderful escapade, the chimney sweep, Tom, meets the water babes in the upper reaches of the River Aire!

Kingsley had every reason to believe that it

was the River Aire which gurgled up at the foot of the Cove, but in fact this is Malham Beck, and the Aire itself begins at the Aire Head Springs. The water which pours out at the foot of the Cove has been traced to a source about three quarters of a mile to the west of Malham Tarn. The dribbling waters have been subjected to courageous diving attempts, but its deeper caves have proved too narrow for human passage after a relatively short seventy feet or so of exploration.

Actually, it seems that the dispute as to the source of these Malham waters is by no means settled. Malham Tarn, 1,250 feet above sea level, and about three miles north of Malham, is regarded by some as the ultimate source. However, the waters from the Tarn, and indeed from other sources, vanish underground before reaching the top of the Cove, and the curious thing is that the waters from the Tarn arrive below Malham village much more quickly (even though it is a greater distance) than the streams emerge at the foot of the Cove. It has been suggested that this delay is due to the extensive pot-holes and syphons which must be negotiated by the waters as they descend the inner caves.

On the very top of the Cove where you might

expect to find springy grass or heather as everywhere else on the Yorkshire moors, you find instead a series of limestone 'pavements'. These are the famous clints, which are supposed to be white (and are generally indeed described in the guidebooks as being white), but which are usually a dark brown due to the layers of mud which are carried over them by the numerous tourists and walkers who flock to the area.

These clints – which are perhaps more famous than they deserve to be, in comparison with others within the area – mark the early stages in the dissolving of limestone by the weakly acidic rainwater flow. The deep depressions between the 'pavement' clints are the grykes, which will in time form vertical caves. At the moment the clints are two to three feet wide, with grykes which are at the most a foot or so wide, and a few yards deep. But for all their inherent strangeness, the real wonder of these limestone pavements of Malham is their dramatic setting, at the edge of the precipice of the Cove, surrounded by quite stunning panoramas.

Some call the grykes 'pots', but it seems that these formations have slightly different origins, the latter being formed by the action of streams, the former by rain. It is easy to visualize the way in which a good pot (such as is found at the Buttertubs) can be cut out of the surrounding stacks of clints by the constant swirl of water around them.

Although it is a phenomenon which few people have actually witnessed, these pavements, and the Cove below, are at times the scene of a most extraordinary inundation of waters. After abnormal rainfalls the Cove becomes one vast and short-lived waterfall, during which moments it must surely be the most amazing sight in the whole of the British Isles. A record of just such a fall of waters, written at the end of the eighteenth century, describes how the huge Tarn, unable to receive

the overflux of rainwaters, overflowed in 'a large and heavy torrent, making a more grand and magnificent cascade than imagination can form an idea of'. The Yorkshire guide, Thomas Howson, also records that the swollen waters of the Tarn have flooded twice in the last forty years, but in each case, the overflood was rapid, being 'dispersed in one vast cloud of spray before it reached the bottom'. He also indicates something of the scale of this miraculous display when remarking that those fortunate enough to witness it 'could not approach within a hundred yards at the foot of the rock without being drenched through'.

Wordsworth was moved to write a sonnet on Malham Cove, albeit not one of his best. The lasting trace of sadness in the poet during his later years made him see the 'vast theatric structure' as the unfinished work of giants, who would have completed the sweep into a perfect round. This feeling must have come from the poet himself, rather than from the magnificent Cove, for there is nothing sad or drear about this structure which conjures giants for Wordsworth, chimney sweeps for Kingsley, and sheer amazement even from those who keep their fantasy nearer to the earth. No giants, but that incomparable artist, Nature, worked and works upon this magnificent display.

The Norber Erratics

The Norber scenery is characterised by the blocks of sandstone which lie upon, and indeed litter the limestone surface. The sandstone is of Silurian Age and is therefore older than the limestone upon which it sits...

Peter R Rodgers

Norber Moor is one of the unsung glories of Yorkshire. It is perhaps so little known because of its proximity to the famous Ingleborough and Pen-y-ghent, those two sentinels of the western dales, each of which thrusts well over two thousand feet of alternating shales, grits and limestone high above the moors within sight of Norber. Norber Moor, although it is less well known, is the setting for two of the most fascinating geological formations in England – a series of clints, and a variety of boulder erratics.

In Yorkshire any mention of clints usually brings to mind that most famous stretch on the head of Malham Cove, yet for all their unique placing on the edge of a precipice, these are by no means as impressive as the clints around this area of Norber, or the series above Kingsdale, which offer a magnificent view of Ingleborough. The Norber clints are more extensive, and have not been covered by the same deposits of brown clay from the boots of walkers and tourists, as have their counterparts of Malham. One can spend hours of welcome solitude on the moors and hills in the area, and it is possible to pass a whole day on Norber Moor without meeting more than a handful of people.

The Norber clints are of a brilliant white limestone, with deep clefts, or grykes, eroded by acidic water seepage into the beds. A most fascinating sight are the natural clints on the western side of Norber, to the west of Robin Proctor's Scar – from which, legend has it, a drunken farmer of this name plunged himself and his horse to an early death. Here natural forms merge almost imperceptibly with the man-made walls of limestone, designed to limit the wanderings of sheep. The clints here are so extensive that one has the feeling of standing upon a petrified sea.

Norber Moor is approximately a mile north-east of the village of Clapham, itself set against Ingleborough Mountain. If you make your way to Robin Proctor's Scar from the direction of Clapham, you must pass through the sloping

Left above: Some of the clints on the top of Robin Proctor's Scar on the edge of Norber Moor, merging with the white dry-stone walls built by man.

Left: The distinctive undulation of Pen-y-ghent which protects the western dales beyond Norber Moor.

Right: The limestone clint pavements at the top of Norber are among the most beautiful and extensive in England.

fields which are the site of the second collection of wonders in this area – the Norber erratics in the rough pastureland beyond Thwaite Lane. These erratics appear to be formed from Silurian slates and sandstones, and were carried to the slopes by glacial movements about eleven thousand years ago. For centuries these boulders lay embedded within the hardened flows of ice which had carried them in its steam-roller motion. When the coming of milder climates melted the ice, the sandstones were gently deposited on top of the limestone which underlies the moors.

Eventually, as the whole surface of the limestone was eroded by wind and rain, the areas of softer chalk around the erratics were levelled down – though the areas immediately beneath the boulders were of course protected by the huge boulders themselves. In this way the erosion made for each of the erratics a little platform, or socle, which at present time bear the main erratics some twelve or fifteen inches above the general landscape level.

The presence of these lovely stones upon such bases, and the total contrast in dark warm colours which they offer against the white limestone, inevitably led to their being regarded by our forebears not so much as geological wonders as geological mysteries. However, the field-work of the Swiss geologist, Louis Agassiz, in the middle of the last century, showed that the origin of all such erratics was glacial movements. Yet, even in the face of such a convincing theory, it is easy to believe that these erratics were dropped carefully on their socles by gigantic hands.

Left and right: Two of the many erratics in the lower reaches of Norber Moor. The difference between the texture and colour of the rock and its underlying white socle puzzled people before the theory of glacial movements was accepted.

Old Harry Rock

... the windy, sousing, thwacking, basting, scourging Jack Ketch of a corner called Old-Harry Point, which lay about halfway along their track, and stood, with its detached posts and stumps of white rock, like a skeleton's lower jaw ...

Thomas Hardy

Once upon a time the chalk ridge of the Purbeck Downs continued across to the Isle of Wight. Comparatively recently – in geological time – the sea eroded this ridge, creating the Isle of Wight, and the Needles, those stumps of the lost chalk bridge which reach out from the island. At the northern point of Swanage Bay on the mainland the chalk cliffs of Ballard Point still thrust vertically up to 380 feet. A mile to the east, along the ridge, are the long peninsula and stacks called Old Harry Rocks, the tallest of which is Old Harry himself. The stacks are the mainland remains of that ancient chalk ridge which stretched to the Isle of Wight, and are visibly being eroded in our day.

On a serene day, with the waves rolling languidly towards this knife-edge promontory, it is difficult to understand why this stack should be given the name 'Old Harry'. It is as though storms are required to make sense of the name, for 'Old Harry' is a familiar and polite name for the Devil. The name may well have appealed, too, because of the meaning of the verb, to harry – to lay waste, to plunder or pillage – which would be appropriate for this devastated scenery.

Old Harry now stands alone off the chalk promontory, but until 1896 he had a tall wife, who was thrown down in a severe gale. When Thomas Hardy gave his romantic descriptions of this coastline in his 'comedy in chapters', *The Hand of Ethelberta*, the two stacks were still together: 'The precipice was still in view, and before it several huge columns of rock appeared, detached from the mass behind. Two of these were particularly noticeable in the grey air – one vertical, stout and square, the other slender and tapering. They were individualized as husband and wife by the coast men. The waves leapt up their sides like a pack of hounds; this, however, though fearful in its boisterousness, was nothing to the terrible games that sometimes went on round the knees of those giants in stone.'

The dramatic peninsula of chalk from which the stack of Old Harry was detached. On a windless day the knife-edge bridge between the land mass and the bulbous peninsula head can be negotiated and Old Harry seen from close proximity.

The danger and wildness is not merely to be experienced out to sea. This pencil-thin promontory stretches its mutilated finger out from the headland, as though reaching across the few yards of waves to the eroded stack of Old Harry. It is a dangerous piece of chalk, not merely because it is slippery and eroded, the grass tufts scarcely gripping its surface, but because the knife-edge is exposed to the winds. Even a slight breeze can make for real danger. I write with some feeling about this, for at one time I had the idea of taking a picture of Old Harry from the stub of headland, and rashly tried to edge across the knife-edge on a wet and windy day. Only the angels saved me, and I did not get the pictures. Fortunately, the views from the safety of the headland spur are superb, especially if one moves to the south, from where one can take in an image of the stack itself.

This land-view should be emphasized because the sheer poetry of Hardy's pen has persuaded many that the cliffs, caves and stacks may be seen at their best only by boat. The most persuasive passage is taken from a description of a sea voyage along the Dorset coast in a steamboat called the *Spruce*. It is so beautiful a piece of literature as to deserve quoting in full: 'The direction and increase of the wind had made it necessary to keep the vessel still further to sea on their return than in going, that they might clear without risk the windy, sousing, thwacking, basting, scourging Jack Ketch of a corner called Old-Harry Point, which lay about halfway along their track, and stood, with its detached posts and stumps of white rock, like a skeleton's lower jaw, grinning at British navigation. Here strong currents and cross currents were beginning to interweave their scrolls and meshes, the water rising behind them in tumultuous heaps, and slamming against the fronts and angles of cliff, whence it flew into the air like clouds of flour. Who could not believe that the roaring abode of chaos smiled in the

sun as gently as an infant during the summer days not long gone by, every pinnacle, crag, and cave returning a double image across the glassy sea.'

Hardy's wild sea has been propitiated in a nearby church. The fine cliff-walk to the Old Harry Rocks takes one close to the village of Studland, where there is a most perfect Norman church, with a choice collection of grotesque stone faces and figures. The entire church is dedicated to the patron saint of sailors, St Nicholas of Myra, who, while popular in Italian images, is more rare in England. (In his other guise, as Nicholas of Bari, he was also the prototype of Santa Claus.) Nicholas was reputed to calm with a word the very tempests which the devil might raise, and this church might be seen as a balance to the effect of that devil, Old Harry, on the other side of the headland. Imagination further suggests that the Agglestone at Studland, which was supposed to have been thrown there from the Isle of Wight by the Devil, was intended for this protective Church of St Nicholas, but missed!

Perhaps the most romantic stretch of the wonderful Dorset coastline is the mile or so which undulates from the magnificent Lulworth Cove (where the poet Keats wrote his last sonnet during his last day in England) to the

Durdle Door. This panorama of chalk is best studied from the sea, from which the pillars of rocks, and the caves of Stair Hole and Cathedral Cavern, can also be seen most clearly.

About a mile west beyond Lulworth Cove, and less than an hour's walk up the steep cliff paths, is the magnificent natural sea-arch called the Durdle Door, virtually a circular arch of mediaeval proportions, as high as it is wide, in a circumference of forty feet. The name of this natural formation has an appropriate etymology, for both 'Durdle' and 'Door' are words from an archaic root meaning 'water'. The door of the Durdle leads from the sea into Dorset, another name associated with the ancient word for water.

Towards Lulworth Cove can be found the fossilized remains of a forest, with hollow stumps large enough to hold five or six people in comfort, an area described by the traveller Arthur Mee as 'one of the natural wonders of the world'. This fossil forest tells us something of the land as it would have appeared at the close of the reptile epoch, perhaps ten million years ago. The chief trees, giant cyads, from which these stone stumps were fashioned, were engulfed with dirt, later buried by clay and limestone, and then re-emerged from ancient seas. What a drama of stone is here!

Peak Cavern

Castleton is famous for the underground limestone caverns in its neighbourhood. The nearest of these, Peak Cavern, was one of the Seven Wonders of the Peak.

Francis R Banks

The cleft called the Devil's Hole which forms the entrance to Peak Cavern is said to be the largest cave entrance in the world. It is a savage gash some sixty feet high, twice as wide, and 330 feet deep in the side of the limestone cliffs which balance Peveril Castle, and leads to a cave system which, however, does not measure up to this promise of size.

The Devil's Hole is such a large aperture that for centuries it was used as a workshop for rope-making, and within its gaping mouth were built rudimentary dwellings to house the workers. Early engravings show the layout of this underground village, with its terraces designed for rope twisting, below which the traveller Karl Philipp Moritz perceived a number of large wheels, on which 'these human moles, the inhabitants of the cavern, make ropes'. Such prints of this strange community virtually depict an ideal village life, but I suspect that they romanticize a great deal. Contemporary descriptions refer to them as being more like sties, with crudely thatched roofs, rather than the well-built, chimneyed structures we see in such pictures. The rope-making is now ended, and only a few relics of machinery remain.

The young poet, Byron, came here as a tourist with one of his many lady-loves. He left us a fine description of how in those days they had to enter the main system of caves behind the Devil's Hole by way of a punt (perhaps straw-covered) pushed by a ferryman, 'a sort of Charon, who wades at the stern, stooping all the time'.

When Queen Victoria visited the cave in 1842, she too would have been ferried into the sixty-foot-high chamber beyond. The way has now been made easy for the tourists by judicious blasting with explosives – easy, perhaps, but less romantic, as is the way of such things.

The cave system leads for a mile or so into the hill, with the ever-present swish of the river waters around and the occasional random dropping of water from above. The formations within the system have little of the beauty or appeal that can be seen in the nearby cave of Treak, and indeed the most lovely of the stalactite formations, surrounded by exquisite flow-stones, is in the back roof of the cavern entrance itself.

Yet, what nature has failed to supply within these caverns and chambers, the human faculty of mythologizing has augmented. The larger cavern within the system was said to have been used as a banquet hall by mediaeval beggars and the king of this horde was supposed to invite the Devil himself to sup, paralleling the wishes of Don Juan. Ben Jonson gave us doggerel verse about these annual suppers:

> Cock Laurel would have the Devil his guest
> And bid him home to the peak to dinner
> Where the fiend never had such a feast
> Prepared in the charge of a sinner.

This link with the Devil is echoed in the names of many of the formations within the caves – perhaps as a sop to tourism – for we find Pluto's Dining Room, the Devil's Cellar, the Styx, and so on. Yet, there are even more references to the Gentleman in older names for the cave: one was Old Horney's Cave, and the other, coined, no doubt, by local Yorkshiremen who mixed no words, was the Devil's Arse. In the thirteenth century Gervase of Tilbury probably had this in mind when he claimed that stormy winds would at times issue from this cleft.

Such demonic legends extended into everyday conversation. Stories are told of a goose which once fell into the cave down the deep pot-hole of Eldon Hole. When it waddled out three days later, its feathers were singed – no one doubted, but by the fires of hell! Charles Leigh, who wrote a fine natural history of the Peak District, called Eldon Hole 'a terrible chasm', and it seems that the same diabolic imagery is connected with the name, for it is almost certainly from the old Saxon *helan*, meaning 'deep hole', from which we have our own modern word 'Hell'. Legend tells that Dudley,

that favourite of Queen Elizabeth I, lowered an unfortunate peasant into this peak hole, and he came up insane, to 'die still mad a few days later'.

When you stand before the dominant Castle Hill, at the straggle end of the village beyond Goosehill Bridge, having crossed waters which have fed through two cave systems, look up towards this gigantic cleft over the rooftops. The Peak Cavern gorge of sheer rock walls, sheathed in ferns and trees, topped by the romantic castle of Peveril, is a sight which can easily conjure a sense of gloom and foreboding if not images of the Devil.

Left: One of the more remarkable flowstone displays, high in the roof of the cavern mouth.

Below: Over the rooftops the dramatic cleft opening of Peak Cavern, topped by the remains of Peveril Castle.

73

Roche

On its own this massive rock would surely qualify as one of the wonders of the Cornish world, but what makes it seem even more fantastic is the mediaeval hermitage which appears to grow out of the rock itself.

R Davidson

The crags of Roche are rather like the remains of jagged meteorites which have plummeted to the earth. It is an eerie lunar landscape, touched by the redemptive powers of the tiny chapel that nestles in the towering pinnacles of rock which, at their highest point, stretch some hundred feet above the surrounding land.

The rocks contrast strangely with the man-made hills to the south which are the stark by-products of the china clay mines. Yet, these two different kinds of mounds are related, since both are essentially made from the same granite substance. The rock is called 'schorl' (not a specifically Cornish name, in spite of what a few guidebooks say), which is a black variety of tourmaline, a dark rock in which nature loves to weave a fantastic strain of sculpture. The mini-mountains of Roche are outcroppings of this hard granite, reaching high into the air like spikes, while the china clay is itself mainly decomposed granite, spread throughout and beneath much of the land north of St Austell, surfacing in bizarre formations as mountains of quartz and other mining rejects, as though in imitation of the natural outcroppings of Roche.

The granite chapel, which clings so tenaciously to the rocks, is as near in spirit and colour to the crags as to make it appear a natural formation of the granite. Nature is slowly claiming this derelict building for her own, and ivy is spreading into the crevices of massive granite blocks, gradually inching them out of place, while wind and rain have already removed the roof, and parts of the topmost walls.

Why was this chapel built, for whom and when? History places it in the fifteenth century, and tells us that it is a hermit cell, dedicated to St Michael, the archangel, who receives the new-released souls at death. Legend, however, makes mockery of this simple history, as is the way with Cornish tales. We are told that John Tregeagle sought sanctuary here from his dreadful penance. But sanctuary for this fearful being was not easy to find. He could neither

Far left: Securely gripping the highest of the rock protuberances is the tiny fifteenth-century hermitage dedicated to St Michael. It has two floors, one formerly used as a dwelling, the other as a chapel.

Left: Two of the strange grey outcrops at Roche rising above the ferns.

receive the Holy Blessing of the hermit within, nor stand the punishment of the devils without, who swarmed above the outcroppings of Roche. For days the racket of his torment continued, until the holy man took pity on his condition, and removed him to the north of Cornwall, where he is still faced with the awful task of making ropes from shifting sands.

Ask a group of Cornishmen who John Tregeagle was, and you will get a variety of answers. He was a giant; in pagan times, he was a chieftain of the early race of Cornishmen; he was an evil spirit, a demon. He was a hated steward of Landhydrock, who came to a pact with the Devil, and was condemned to empty the bottomless brooding waters of Drozmary Pool (that Dead Sea of Bodmin Moor) with a sieve-like shell ... Whatever or whoever the original John Tregeagle was, his name is still associated with the crags and chapel of Roche.

Some historians ignore the French origin of

Some of the outcrops seen from the plateau of Roche, looking north.

the word Roche, and insist that the curious name was derived from a Roche, who was himself from Montpelier, and who came to live in these outcroppings, first as a hermit, and later as a victim of the plague which he had helped to combat in this area. He was terribly disfigured by this illness, and the story has a dog bring him a loaf of bread to his cell every day. But this part of the story is an old tale, told in many different lands, and it is certainly older than the Michael Chapel and the cell of this Cornish Roche.

The view from the topmost walls of the chapel will remind us that many of the natural wonders of Cornwall are found underground. From this lofty perch (the anchorite cell is

actually below the chapel in this two-storey building) we can look southwards, towards the lunar landscape of the clay workings, eastwards towards the rugged Helman Tor, and westwards over towards the town of St Dennis (who was probably no local saint at all, but merely a name of recent corruption from the Cornish word *dinas*, meaning 'fort'). But most impressive of these views are those of the clay mine (quarry) remains. The finest deposits of china clay in the earth are still mined here, and are likely to be excavated for many years to come, leaving even more white pyramids throughout the land. Yet the spirit-infested pinnacles of Roche will outlast even these man-made mountains.

The outcrop carrying the hermitage dominates Roche. From the roofless chapel there are very impressive views towards the clay-mining deposits in the south.

St Michael's Mount

And we came to the Isle of Flowers, their breath
* met us out on the seas,*
For the Spring and the middle Summer sat each
* on the lap of the breeze.*
            Alfred Lord Tennyson

'Sometimes it is like a faint shadow; sometimes white in the sun; at times it darkens under a passing cloud. Always present, except when the sea-mist hides it, its mystery never goes. In calm or storm its granite walls are like a fortress rising from the sea.' Like any travel writer, Arthur Mee must fumble for words and phrases to capture the beauty and mystery of this place, the most singular site of Cornwall. The setting for the island, which Tennyson called 'the Isle of Flowers', is alone quite splendid, enfolded in a great sweep of bay from the Lizard to Lamorna Cove.

The mount is perhaps best seen for the first time from the hill to the east, from where it appears like a castle out of a courtly romance surrounded by a sea-moat, perhaps rendered more mysterious by the westerly setting of the sun. It is over two hundred feet high, a mile in circumference, and some twenty-one acres in extent.

A less imaginative view of the mount can be had from the beach of Mount Bay itself, from among the granite rocks which introduce a wild foreground, but show indeed that the mount is no man-made castle, as the magic of the setting sun would have one believe. It is, in fact, a natural fortress upon which man has lodged for a while a cluster of buildings, with a proficiency and taste which for once adorns and completes nature, rather than deforms it. From here one can see that the mount is about a third of a mile out to sea, with a harbour, pier and houses gathered around the castle, from which rocks appear to pour forth, rather than lend it support.

The history of this mount echoes the history of England. Mount Bay was once upon a time (and hardly so long ago by geological time) no bay at all, for areas now covered by the sea contain signs of old forests and peoples. Primitive human stone axes were certainly made on what is now sea-mud bottom, less than four thousand years ago. Perhaps it was the same sea-rise, or even an earth-tilt, which permitted the waters to make the Mount an island, that also covered the fabled land of Lyonesse, that ancient land off the end of Cornwall. St Michael's Mount emerges (no doubt with a different name, for then there were other gods to propitiate) from the mists of mythology with the giant Cormoran who lived on it, or built it, as the various legends claim. It was also the first place in England to be christianized.

Left: The Mount at sunset, from the eastern mainland.

Above: St Michael's Mount seen from the rocky shingle of Mount Bay.

Christianity came to Cornwall by way of the Mediterranean traders (or, as some would have us believe, by way of the Romans), and, as the later Saxons did not penetrate Cornwall to any great extent, the ancient rites were adhered to, and as such surprised the later evangelizing Christians who spread the gospel from the mainland of England in later centuries.

The island was dedicated to St Michael, because some Cornish fishermen of the sixth century had seen him in a vision. Pilgrims for centuries afterwards flocked to the spot and eventually, by 1044, a Benedictine Priory was founded on the island. (Milton wrote a personal version of this story in his *Lycidas*, attributing great vision to a hermit who lived there.)

It was still a venerated island when Edward the Confessor made it over as a gift to the Abbey of St Michel, on the Normandy coastline – a gift perhaps encouraged by the resemblance the two mounts bear to one another. There was a rising in 1425, and as a result the island became a military fortress. During the rebellion of Warbeck, at the time of the Wars of the Roses, resistance was offered: Sir John Arundel lost his life on these rocks, fighting the Lancastrians, and his body is still within the chapel precinct. In turn the Mount became a Royalist stronghold (after the Restoration Charles II dined there) and an elegant private island for the nobility, and so it remained until Lord St Levan gave it to the National Trust in 1954.

The Seven Sisters

Beachy Head, a popular place for suicides, has a sublimity about it, particularly when seen from the sea ... the Belle Toute Lightship was built on a rocky promontory west of the Head – to have built it on top would have been useless because in days of low cloud it would have been obscured in vapour ...

John Seymour

The Seven Sisters, with the undulations of Raven Brow, Short and Rough Brow, Bran Point and Flagstaff Point.

The panoramic chalk face which sweeps its dizzy beauty in gentle undulations towards the massive headland of Beachy Head near Eastbourne, is called the Seven Sisters. Until fairly recently the Seven Sisters had seven brothers. These were called the Seven Charles – even earlier, the Seven Carls – and were sea stacks left behind as the vertical undulations of chalk retreated under the sea's erosion. The last of these succumbed to the waves in 1853. It is a sobering thought to realize how quickly landscapes around us are changing – these chalk cliffs looked very different to the invading Romans, or even to the Normans, a mere thousand years ago!

Anyone standing before these cliffs might reasonably assume that the name for the eastern headland, 'Beachy Head', is descriptive of the lovely shingle beach which edges up along the miles of sheer verticals of white. The assumption would be quite wrong, however, for the name is a corruption of the French *beau chef*, a name given to this tallest of the southern English headlands by the Normans.

The Seven Sisters stretch luxuriantly from Cuckmere Haven in the west to Birling Gap in the east. On their green heads the grasses sweep up and down in a soft undulation, but to the south the cliffs drop in sheer white to a depth of 575 feet. Their names often preserve fragments of ancient languages, starting in the west with Haven Brow, which was corrupted into Raven Brow. This first headland hardly resembles a bird's brow, unless such brows be sharp verticals, but the name may be connected with that of Cuckmere Haven on the nearby river mouth.

Then follows the unimaginatively named pair Short Brow and Rough Brow, which appear to have no topographical truth in their names, and may be related to early sounds with meanings now lost. Bran Point comes next, a name which was also given to the Celtic god of the underworld. Flagstaff Point seems painfully modern, and one wonders what ancient term it may have displaced.

Bail's Hill and Went Hill Brow complete the series with a French flourish: Bail's Hill is sometimes called Baily's Hill, and this is sufficient to give its meaning away, for it mutely speaks of a castle and its bailey; not surprisingly, there are indeed remains of an ancient hill fort upon the headland nearby. Went Hill is clearly an English-seeming corruption of the French, *vent*, 'wind', a name which is for once appropriate in terms of its climate.

There are, then, seven of these females with largely masculine names, as there are seven stars in the constellation of the Pleiades, which is also called the Seven Sisters. The number

seven has magical connotations and the ancients were fond of grouping things into sevens. This they would often do with a certain amount of duplicity or dexterity, for they claimed 'seven seas', despite the fact that there were only five in the original lists, and so they divided the Atlantic and the Pacific into north and south to make the full quota. Such juggling was required in an age when there was still felt to be something magical in number, when it was believed that there were seven vices, balanced by seven virtues, seven planets, and seven archangels, and that man himself was composed of seven natures dwelling within the seven different substances of being! So one might perhaps suspect some adjustment in the counting of the Seven Sisters, and indeed there is, for there are really eight cliffs! The eighth is modestly called Flat Hill – yet the Sisters remain seven in the popular mind.

The dips between the green undulations which top the white switchback show that at one time rivers flowed seawards and carved these gentle valleys. The whole chalk face of the Seven Sisters is a splendid cross-section display of an ancient past.

Behind the name of Seven Sisters there is a delicate feeling for the spiritual purity, the cosmic appropriateness, of this beautiful place. The name itself is a silent support to the claim that this line of cliffs is a wonder of the material world.

Treak Cavern
and Winnats Pass

This cavern ... rivals those of Cheddar in the profuse display of scores of stalactites and the attendant stalagmitic formations ... The most remarkable characteristic of the hill in which it is situated, known as Treak Cliff, is that it is the only place in the world where Blue John stone is found.

R J W Hammond

Winnats Pass, seen from the hillside which is penetrated by the cave system of Treak Cavern.

Winnats Pass in the Peak District is one of the most lovely of natural passes in the whole of Britain. It is walled by steep green and white striations of grasses and limestone, a gorge which was first cut by glacial actions, and then later rounded by rains and winds to its present distinctive shape. It has the appearance of being modelled from the limestone, as though careful artistic hands have worked at its making, rather than being gouged and pressed out by the terrible upheavals of the earth.

The road which has been engineered strip-like through the bottom of the pass has not really destroyed its beauty, but affords a standard by which the breathtaking proportions may be perceived. A walk on the wide pavements of grasses alongside the climb of this road permits a wonderful view of the whole of the gorge-pass, but the finest fixed panoramic view is that to be had from the hillock to the right of the pass entrance, beyond Castleton.

When, in the thirteenth century, the literary monk, Gervase of Tilbury, described the nearby Peak Cavern, he spoke of the storm winds which actually arose within the cavern to blow into the world beyond. This curious idea has been literally repeated in many guidebooks as the monk's fantasy, or even as an explanation of the bawdy names given to the Peak Cavern in less delicate times. Yet it could perhaps have been a slip of memory on the part of Gervase. If he visited the cave, or even knew the area at all, then he could not fail to have seen Winnats Pass, which is actually on one side a continuation of the Castle Hill, above the cavern. Gervase must have known that the original meaning of Winnats is from the compound Old English words *wind geat*, meaning 'gap through which the wind sweeps' – an idea quite easily projected to the nearby cave.

Winnats Pass is more than the old name might imply – more than a mere gateway for the winds – for beneath its limestone walls are some of the most spectacular caves in the world.

Indeed, the claim of Winnats Pass to being a wonder rests more upon what it hides than upon its external appearance, incredibly beautiful as this is.

The most impressive of these internal wonders is Treak Cavern, which has been bored by rainwater and streams into the far side of Winnats Pass. This cave has a character quite unlike that of the threatening gash which announces the entrance to Peak Cavern. Here the entrance would be scarcely noticed, were it not for the tourist accommodations, for it is a slight opening and halfway up the steep hill – now reached by a sharp climb of concrete steps. Once inside the contrasts are more pronounced, for there is a wealth of forms such as are found in few British caves.

The ancient fame of the Treak Caverns rested in the first instance upon the wonderful veins of Blue John stones (which are still worked in winter time, when tourist pressure in the show-caves is not so strong). This stone is unique to the Peak District, and has been mined since at least Roman times. For this reason parts of the cave were known to many early travellers. However, this early series of caves was by no means the most beautiful which nature has carved into the limestone of Winnats. A much more extensive system was discovered by accident in 1926, and the cave is still divided into the old and the new series.

The old series was obviously known in pre-historic times, since Bronze Age skeletons have been found here, and it is also within this series that the worked seams of Blue John are found. This lovely rare mineral is not merely blue, but consists mainly of blue and yellow/brown striations. It is probably from this colour combination that the curious name has arisen, for in the French of the Normans who prized and mined the stones, its colour would have been termed *bleu-jaune*, 'blue-yellow', a name most easily corrupted into the present English form. John Royse tells us in *The Geology of Castleton,* however, that the name was given in contradistinction to a metal-blend known to the old miners as Black Jack. He is of the opinion that this unique Blue John is a result of water deposits within the caves.

In the cave series which bears the Blue John stones there is also one of the finest stalactite displays in England. This is a wall in the appropriately named Dream Cave, where the stuff of dreams is fenced in by ordinary chicken wire, in order to stave off the depredations of the stalactite hunters. In this display one can study the slow union between a hanging stalactite and a rising stalagmite, which will eventually forge a single column. At the present time the two are separated by about one and a half inches, a gap which should be bridged in less than five centuries.

The finest cave display within the new series is Aladdin's Cave. These systems are 'show-caves', which is to say that access to them has been made as easy as possible, and they have been well-lighted – even stage-managed, to some extent. This lighting tends to emphasize the yellow qualities within the calcite deposits, yet their natural colours are themselves of delicate and various hues. In particular the iron trace elements work a magic with the white of the calcite to produce subtle purples, reds and oranges. Other metal and organic traces have given blues, greens and many different colours, almost all of them subdued by the dominant yellow of the lighting.

Thomas Hobbes wrote of the Seven Wonders of the Peak, and included the neighbouring Peak Cavern, impressed no doubt by the savage cleft at the entry to the caves. I can only assume that he had never visited the old series of Treak Cavern, for if he had, then there is no doubt in my mind that he would have chosen this as one of the seven wonders of the Peak District, if not of Great Britain itself.

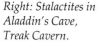
Right: Stalactites in Aladdin's Cave, Treak Cavern.

Right: Another view of Aladdin's Cave. The protective wire mesh is designed to foil the stalactite souvenir hunter.

White Scar Caves

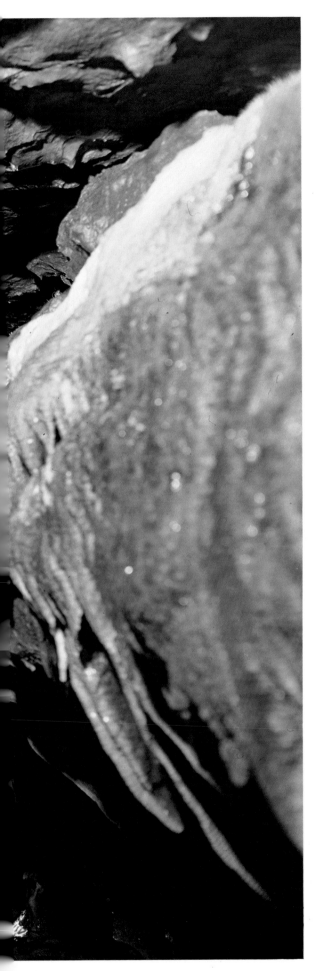

In only the last million or so years ... glaciers swept over the whole region and moulded the landscape we observe today; and during the warmer periods between the individual glaciations, water flowed through the limestone and formed the caves.

A C Waltham

The three peaks of the Yorkshire moors – Whernside, Ingleborough and Pen-y-ghent – owe their distinctive silhouettes to the geological structure of this part of the world. They are virtually horizontal layers of grits and shales standing on an undulating limestone bed. Beautiful as they are, even more magnificent sights lie buried beneath them, for here, in the bowels of the earth, are a thousand or so caves which have been cut by underground streams and rivers into the limestone. Ingleborough, for example, enfolds within its 2,373 feet the extraordinary Ingleborough Cave, with quarter-mile chambers of stalactites and stalagmites. Nearby is the magnificent Gaping Gill, the largest pothole in Britain, a water-fed chamber which is said to be large enough to swallow York Minster.

The most extraordinary of the caves open to the public view is the series known as the White Scar Caves, at the foot of the White Scars ridge, which slopes 600 feet above the cave entrance in white and green striations of limestone and grasses. Within this series virtually the whole range of underground formations is gathered: there is a complete display of stalagmites and stalactites, a running stream, two remarkable waterfalls and a large number of other unique structures.

The discovery of the system is a romance in itself, for the cave was first penetrated by a student from Cambridge University called Christopher Long, in 1923. Long had with him only the most primitive equipment, yet he managed to struggle beyond the second waterfall, and into the gallery which still bears his name. A later visit, in the company of potholing friends, took him as far as the underground lakes, and these he swam, in ice-cold waters, his passage dubiously lighted by candles stuck on his helmet.

The show-cave which is a result of this exploration extends for half a mile to some 600 feet below the surface, but even now the caves

The furthermost reaches of the show-cave in the White Scar system, where a varied display of flowstones and stalactites hang above the underground stream.

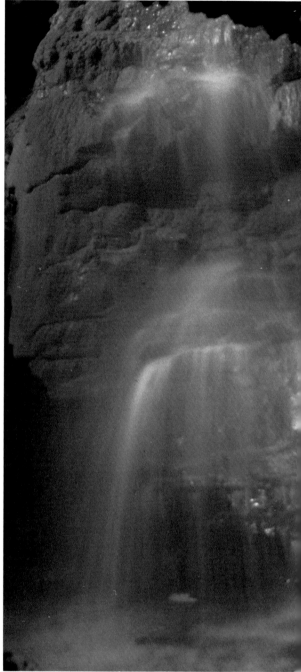

beyond have not yet been fully explored. Surveys have extended the system a further three miles (still not open to the public), and it is believed that the caves extend for about five miles to link up with that other wonder of the Yorkshire Dales – Gaping Gill.

Within the show sections of the cave, one can form a picture of just how the continual action of water creates such caves. Even those not trained in geology will be able to appreciate the way in which during millions of years water erosion of the limestone has carved tunnels with hard floors which rest upon the less easily eroded black slate. This erosion is visibly acting on a magnificent scale through the waterfalls.

Underground waterfalls in show-caves are relatively rare things, and the two in White Scar Caves are undoubtedly among the finest in the country. Inside these systems the roar of the falls is always present in the background; indeed the noise from these twelve-foot cascades helps one appreciate the extent to which the cave acoustics magnify sound. I have been privileged to spend some hours alone in the caves – a quite extraordinary experience, not merely because of the beauty of the calcite formations, but because of the very pressure of the noise which peoples the chambers and passages with strange beings. Sometimes there is merely the gurgling of the streams as they flow alongside or beneath one's feet, but always behind this gurgling is the background roar of the waterfalls.

The passages beyond the waterfalls are carved in delicate flow formations by thick deposits of calcite, large areas of which are still being imperceptibly built up by water flows. The pure white calcite is at times exquisitely coloured by red, yellow and green due to impurity deposits. Although some of the green is the result of copper traces within the calcite, on the whole it is caused by algae growth which is encouraged by the warmth of the electric bulbs used to light the caves. A breathtaking display of this multi-coloured calcite grotesque is seen at the barrier at the end of the show-cave, which is constructed upon a bridge of concrete and wood over the bed of a fast-flowing stream, about a quarter of a mile from the entrance. From this point one can study at leisure the stumps of stalagmites, the rich colours of flowstones, and the delicate stalactites which hang from the roof of the cavern beyond.

In this system calcium carbonate deposits, dripping and accumulating from the roof, form stalactites of two essentially different forms. One has a hollow centre, encouraging the growth of long straw stalactites, beautiful displays of which are within the caverns beyond the show-caves; while the other is the more

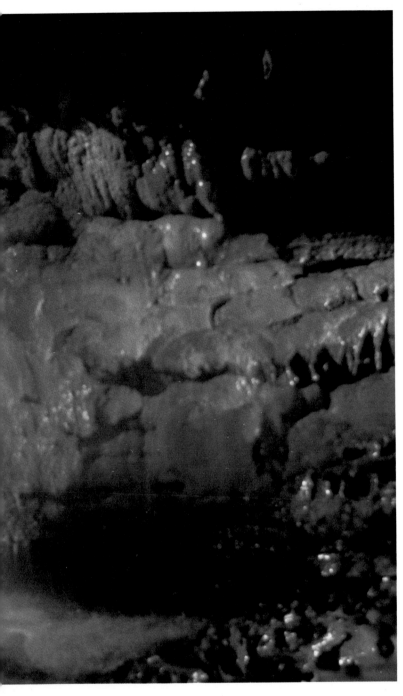

tunnelled after the last extensive glaciation of the area.

Beyond the colourful display at the end of the show-cave are many further wonders of nature, all set against the never-ending display of the white-base calcite flows. The first of these wonders is the second lake, which is two hundred feet long, and on average seven feet deep, the roof above pressing very closely to the water surface. The only way to get across is by swimming – which no doubt explains why the public show-cave section ends where it does. Beyond this lake is one of the largest underground chambers in the country, some three hundred feet long, fifty feet wide, and rising to forty feet.

One very interesting geological feature at White Scar is the fact that the caves appear to grope upwards for light and air, some five miles in from the entrance under the Scar itself. These holes are really inlets created by streams from above working their way through the limestone and discharging into the main cave, to merge with the other thirty or more feed-streams within the entire system. One of these streams can be seen from the top pouring into a 160-foot shaft called Boggart's Roaring Hole, on the far side of the Great Scar Limestone, almost in the Yoredale Shales.

commonly found conic stalactite with its thick solid chunks. These latter forms sometimes give rise to the most fantastic of all stalactites, the fragile helictites, which have a multitude of arms and feet, all reaching out in many directions, like a petrified Hydra. There is no accurate method of dating the growth of the various calcite formations, but it is generally estimated at one inch every five hundred years. However, the thin straw formations, some of which are five feet long, may grow as much as an inch in a century, and some may have grown to their present lengths in only ten thousand years or so – a mere hiccup in geological time. These dates do link up with the estimated age of the present system, since it is likely that the caves were

Right: A two-foot long stalactite near the entrance to the White Scar show-cave system.

IRELAND

PICTURE: ERRIGAL, COUNTY DONEGAL – SEE PAGE 112

Introduction

I met an American on the Irish roads . . .
'Where do you go?' I asked him. 'Killarney?
*   Tramore? Bundoran?'*
'Nadd in County Cork, Rosegreen in County
*   Tipperary, Modeligo in County Waterford and*
*   Gweedore in County Donegal.'*
'What do you find in these places?'
'Human beings!' he said and went his way
*   whistling.*

                    Bryan MacMahon

When God had the angels build a wall around Paradise, so that man might thereafter be excluded, I think they forgot about Ireland. Ireland is a sort of immense garden, partly cultivated by man, as in the wide open spaces between Dublin and Galway, and partly cultivated by the angels, as in the mountain chains, north and south. Such images are not out of place when one attempts to generalize about this land; you simply could not write or talk in such terms when describing other parts of the British Isles.

One can scarcely write about any part of Ireland without noticing the Christian impulse; there is a monastery on the larger of the Skelligs, a reference to a saint in the ancient name of Errigal, myriad churches, monasteries and crosses which litter the Burren, and many more examples. And yet, older than Christianity is the Irish mythology, which tells of a time when all men were giants, and which has insinuated itself into the rocks and stones of this mystic land: the heroes who strode over the Loop Peninsula or leapt to safety from female guiles, the giants who struggled on the Antrim coast, and the many other creatures human and superhuman who merge and mingle with the landscapes. As you walk up to the topmost part of the cliffs of Moher, you might with reason believe that the slab-stones which protect you from the wind and spray were the works of giants. And when you learn the common Irish name of the nineteenth-century gentleman who had them built to protect you – O'Brien – then you feel little gap between the works of giants and the works of man.

The merging of mythology with nature means that whenever one looks for subjects to write about, many different places beckon. How can one, for example, select from the many islands around the coast? Faced with so many, each special and individual, how can one choose? To cut short argument, therefore, and to explain why the startlingly lovely Aran islands have not

been included, or the intense Blaskets, and a whole medley of other islands, I have quite simply written about the smallest and the largest of them, so as to encompass their full variety and contrast.

The smallest of the 'inhabited' Irish sea islands is the fang rock of Skellig Michael, inhabited now by a lone lighthouse keeper. As well as being a geological wonder in itself, perhaps one of the most remarkable islands in the world, it wears a man-made crown of monastic buildings which speak eloquently and with intense sadness of the real power of Ireland, which lies at the moment in her past. The largest island is Achill, which modern technology has joined with the mainland, so that only the powerful independence of the islanders has been able to prevent the island losing its character. The cliffs of the Menawn alone could justify the choice of Achill, but it is also set with mountains and fantastic beaches.

But amongst the many mountains, how can one possibly justify the inclusion of the mountains of Donegal, and the exclusion of the distinctive peak of Ben Bulben, even if the white magnificence of Errigal is included? I have almost no answer to make. Perhaps I should have dealt in detail with the highest chain of Ireland, the Reeks of Macgillicuddy, but at least they appear in my glance at the Gap of Dunloe, while the beauty of the mountains of Wicklow go unobserved and unpraised because by including Donegal I am able to point to a wider variety of forms and geological structures. In the end the choice is personal and the mountains of the Donegal highlands are to my mind the most lovely in Ireland, with the white peak of Errigal to the north, and the ice-worn summits of the Derryveaghs to the south.

When it came to cliffs, Slieve League had to be omitted, despite its steady, 45-degree decline of 1,972 feet which in statistics at least dwarfs the Cliffs of Moher, which *are* included. The reason is that the Cliffs of Moher are more

Above and right: In the northern areas above Spiddal the landscape of Ireland is of a lunar-like intensity such as is rarely seen in the British Isles. The beauty is fresh and austere, the region little visited by tourists, and yet it is one of the delights of Ireland.

Above and above right: The mist-shrouded top of the beautiful Connor Pass, north of Dingle – grand and breathtaking in the austerity of its natural formations.

Right: The beginning of the northern entry to the Connor Pass, on the Dingle Peninsula.

immediately impressive – longer, with their five miles, if not higher, and certainly more precipitous. Having wandered along many impressive cliffs in Ireland, when I think of Irish cliffs, then it is these at Moher which spring to mind. For that reason alone, these are selected as a wonder, even though it is sad to omit the perpendicular cliffs along the peninsula of Loop Head, some of which are especially striking in their variety of formations – with the dark heaviness of the Rocks of Grania and the magnificent black cliffs adjacent which sweep down vertically into the sea. But at least the beautifully arched sea bridge of Ross, to the north of Loop Head, is too strangely artistic to be left out of any survey of the natural wonders of the country.

Killarney speaks to the heart of all travellers, and is, of course, outstanding in natural scenery, with each lake worthy of a visit, a round trip to be highlighted by the vantage point of Ladies' View, which is quite breathtaking. Yet Killarney offers more than lakes, for it is hedged in by mountains which harbour the dramatic pass of the Dunloe Gap. It is this combination of lakes, mountains and dramatic pass which urges the choice of Killarney from all those possible sites. Yet, even having made this choice, there is an element of regret, for I would

have wished to include within this book a survey of that most dramatic and varied pass in the mountains north of Dingle, the Connor Pass.

For all the basaltic similarities with Staffa, the Giant's Causeway is unique in the four countries. The relatively short walk from Clamshell to Fingal's Cave, over the quiltwork of Staffa's hexagonal columns, is an altogether different experience from that offered by the Causeways of Antrim. These can be explored with all the freedom that small peninsulas, exposed to the elements, permit. I do not know who numbered the 32,000 columns which the three peninsulas are supposed to comprise, but I am sure that it would have taken weeks of counting, whereas the basalts in the pavements of Staffa might possibly be counted in a morning. Comparison is in any case invidious, as the settings are so different – the boom and music of Fingal, even the romantic journey out, are so different from the touristic entrance to the cliff wonders of this coast-line in Antrim; the exploration of the sweep of coast, from the western wonder of Runkerry Cave to the furthest eastern wonder, Benbane Head, or even Dunseverick Castle, is a very different experience from that of the enclosed nature of tiny Staffa. In fairness, it is only the basaltic structure and ancient legends which

The hexagonal
basalts which form
the Giant's
Causeway in
County Antrim.
The curved hollows
have trapped
pockets of receding
tide water.

connect the two places, for they are wonders of a different sort.

The Burren and the Rock Close of Blarney are also unique, without parallels in the other countries. Rock Close has all the expensive feeling of eighteenth-century landscaping about it, and yet its rocks are also shaped to the modern taste; the eighteenth-century eye would not have seen these stones as we do, influenced as we are by the art of Henry Moore and other abstract artists, and aware of many stone circles and standing stones. Certainly there are rock areas more fantastic by far in the other countries – as, for instance, the granite fantasies of Roche – but there is nothing with the exquisite feeling for space and placing as the curious stones

which stand in the shadow of that most famous stone in Ireland, at Blarney Castle.

The Burren is a wide slash of swollen limestone, with a name which sounds fittingly close to 'barren', on the southern coast of Galway Bay. A mediaeval writer might have found an appropriate symbol of earthly unity in the Burren, for its flora and fauna, and indeed its form, are the result of a meeting of the four elements. The grey limestone is the earth, sharply separated from the translucent air of the sky, while the life within its crevices and valleys is supported mainly by the fire-derived warmth of the watery Gulf Stream pouring its months of heat into the massive square miles of limestone, which then acts for the remainder of the year as

the hexagonal columns on the Giant's Causeway, or the ancient rock sentinels on the Skelligs, speak of hidden mysteries. The human senses are rather like the sun for, just as the sun lights up the world and sharpens our vision, yet hides with its glare the stars beyond, so our human senses see the material world in detail, yet miss the real beauties behind. In Ireland, at least, it is harder to forget the spiritual behind the natural forms. And if you do not come too close, at twilight or at dawn, you may even chance upon a leprechaun, catching a sight of his startled face before he whips himself away from the visible world.

The Little Skellig, seen past one of the natural outcrops on Skellig Michael, with the mainland of Ireland in the distance.

an off-peak radiator system.

After travelling the length and breadth of Ireland, I feel rather like the American TV director who came all the way to Ireland to interview a leprechaun. Many of the Irish openly scoffed at him, yet I have seen enough of the natural wonders of this land to know that in a way he was right. He may never have had his interview, but he was right to come in search of one. It could well be a hopeless quest, to search for a leprechaun who is willing to speak in the language of men, but at least the search will keep one travelling through this land, and, while searching for the invisible, one will be tantalized by, at times satiated by, the beauties of its visible natural wonders. The very forms of

Achill Island

I suppose that anyone living in a place which faces as it does the dramatic Menawn Cliffs towering over the lovely Keel Strand would soon lose all sense of time.

Harold Rose

Left: A sea-arch at the foot of the Menawn Cliffs on Achill Island at low tide. This arch is part of a rich cluster of sea-arches which penetrate the massif from several angles, the whole rather like a series of flying buttresses.

Below left: Slievemore seen from the sands below Menawn, across a thin sheet of retreating tidal waters.

Achill Island, the 'Eagle Island' of the ancients, is an island no longer, for it is now joined to mainland County Mayo by a bridge over the Achill Sound. The Irish farmers who work the land beyond the Sound will tell you ruefully that, before the bridge came there were no foxes on Achill, but these cunning creatures slipped over on the bridge and now prowl among their chicken and lambs. 'Before the bridge came' is indeed synonymous for a sort of Irish Golden Age with some of the natives, who savoured their ancient loneliness and now object to their island being the object of a far from religious pilgrimage by the youth of Ireland, who drive and hitch from the other side of Dublin, and even from the mountains of Wicklow, to gather in tents, sleeping bags and pubs for bank-holidays of friendly riot. Yet despite the bridge, which carries foxes and tourists into this wonderland, Achill is an island still in spirit, an island of two vast mountains, cemented together with moors, trimmed by superb cliffs and exquisite sandy beaches.

The famous Atlantic Drive winds its way up and down through this island, from Gloghmore to the west of Achill Sound, and gives stupendous views of sea and earth. The sea works its daily wonders of moods and intensities as it slams into the cliffs or purrs on the sand beaches, while the earth works a slower rhythm and annually gives birth to the explosive rhododendron flowers with their heavy scents.

At Keel, to the south of Achill, is one of the most magnificent beaches to be seen anywhere. The sands are guidebook yellows, set against a backdrop of blue mountains and even bluer sea which look almost too perfect, and at times the skies play at magic with reflections on the wet sands, bathing them with their amethyst sheen. Slievemore, the highest point on the island at 2,204 feet, towers above the sands, which are often flooded with quarter of an inch of water.

However, it is not the mountain of Slieve-more, nor the beach of Keel, which is the most special feature of Achill Island, but the delights of the Menawn Cliffs. The guidebooks will tell you about the height of the Menawn, which is 800 feet, but it is not so much the height which should delight the traveller as the exquisite natural artistry of the lower stretches of the cliff where it edges on to the sea, framing the eastern end of the three miles of sands before Keel. Within the cliffs are a medley of natural forms to delight the eye – sea-stacks and arches, caves and geos, with a profusion of multi-coloured rocks which must be traversed by those in search of the cliff's delights.

As though to outdo other sea-sculptures, one sea-arch, only a hundred yards or so from the beach, has spawned a whole conglomerate of minor arches: no fewer than five, colonnaded like exotic flying buttresses around the main, twenty-foot-high arch, as though the rock supports for the cliffs above were being splintered in preparation for a vast collapse into the waves. Standing away from the cliffs are also sea-stacks – former arches – nowhere very dramatic or enormous, yet beautifully proportioned and perfect in form and hue.

Achill also boasts cliffs said to be the highest sea-cliffs in Ireland at 1,950 feet above sea-level. High as the cliffs at Croaghaun are, however, they are not sheer enough to catch the breath like those at Moher, which are only a third of the height. The view from Croaghaun heights, reached by way of Lough Acorrymore, takes in a panoramic view of Blacksod Bay on the sandy dunes of Mullet to the north, the Nephin Beg Mountains to the east, and south across Clew Bay the lovely distinctive cone of Croagh Patrick, the mountain holy of the Irish, where their saint passed forty days of prayer, fasting through an infestation of demons.

The locals of Achill will no doubt tell you that the Menawn Cliffs are best seen by boat and, indeed, if it is mere height which interests you,

Right: The base of the cliffs at Menawn, full of exotic forms and subtle colours.

Below: The view out to sea from below the Menawn cliffs offers some of the loveliest panoramas in Ireland.

Above: An exotic sea-stack on the shore below Menawn.

then this approach probably does give the best view, for only from a distance can you get the perspective needed to see them properly. However, if you wish to go by boat at all, then choose rather to see the Croaghaun Cliffs, or go round to the north of Slievemore, and visit the Seal Caves, which are in any case accessible only by boat. Those who prefer their wonders by land are strongly advised to resist all temptations to climb either of the three heights offered by Achill Island, and to walk and scramble over the sea-rocks which lie at the foot of the cliffs of Menawn and to the east of the lovely strip of sands at Keel, for here a timeless beauty is to be found, and nature is at her sculptural best.

Right: The cliff edge which used to hold an end of the now destroyed outer-most Bridge of Ross

Far right: The Bridge of Ross seen across the inner natural amphitheatre.

Below: The main Bridge of Ross from the north, looking towards the peninsula of Loop Head.

Bridges of Ross

*A pair of extraordinary arches beneath which the
sea flows into dark, rather sinister pools...*
Eric Newby and Diana Petry

Some three miles before the Loop Peninsula lifts
its head to dizzy heights of geological display,
the sea has made an inroad into the dark
carbonaceous slates to form a geo bridged by
one of the most lovely sea-arches in Ireland.
This formation is still pluralized as the 'Bridges
of Ross', but in truth there is now only one
bridge left. Originally, there were of course two
bridges, but the larger one, which faced on to
the sea, was swept away in a terrible gale a
couple of years ago. However, the remaining
sea-arch which still bridges the long and curving geo may be regarded in its single state as
one of the strangest natural formations in
Ireland.

The bridges were formed when the sea carved
a long and twisting gallery cave into the dark
rock. The roof of this cave fell in at two places,
leaving the two bridges and two long sea-filled
amphitheatres in the rock. The collapse of the
seaward arch is merely the most recent product
of geological movement which has been continuing for millennia. No doubt the remaining
bridge will one day succumb to the waves,
although it is well protected at present from the
sea's fury by the serpentine passage of the geo
which leads to it.

The bridge itself is some 10 yards wide on the
turf-covered top, and has a fall of about 40 feet
to the sea-bed below. To the west are the most
obvious remains of the exposed cave, for here
there is an elongated amphitheatre, some forty
feet deep, with a circumference of about 150
yards. The walls of this amphitheatre, especially
those to the northernmost side, are laid in
perfectly horizontal striations as though by the
trowel of a master craftsman. The arch of the
bridge with its intricately interwoven slabs of
striated rocks shows similar artistic mastery.

In the curiously formed rocks around this
edge of the Loop Peninsula there are a number
of smaller 'bridges', which are really natural
arches worked by the seas into the cliff face. The
most impressive is the one towards the north-

ern point, best reached by walking over the
main bridge and climbing down the curving
undulations of rock strata, almost to the most
northerly point. A walk upon these carved
strata is a real delight – it is more like climbing
over an organic form, for everywhere one sees
rhythms and forms which recall the living
rather than the inorganic dead.

The red, rough and gnarled breaks in the rock
above this small sea-arch indicate the point
where the span of the larger bridge of Ross
began. At times the waves reach right over
these rocks and sweep through the easterly
depression, and in rough weather it is advisable
to admire the main bridge from the sides of the
amphitheatre.

The Burren

Stony, seaboard, far and foreign,
Stony hills poured over space
Stony outcrop of the Burren,
Stones in every fertile place...

                    John Betjeman

'Nothing happens in this blessed place, but a stray beggar or a heron,' wrote W B Yeats from his tower near Gort, on the Burren, where he composed some of his finest poems. Little happens there today, save for the daily and annual rhythms of nature, for the Burren is in spirit and form much like the unchanging surface of the moon, apparently having hardly enough water to slake a man's thirst or even a tree to shelter him from the sun. An earlier and infamous version of this view of the Burren is put into the mouth of one of Cromwell's officers, who saw in this place no trees to hang a man, no water to drown him. In fact, that soldier cannot have looked very far, for the valley rifts in this fifty square miles of limestones have trees in plenty, and the water-laden atmosphere of Ireland creates curious grassy hollows which fill with water during wet weather from the subterranean passages within the limestone, and which are known as *turloughs*. Yet the feeling in almost all parts of the Burren proper is indeed one of desolation and deprivation. On the main coastal road from Kinvarra to Ballyvaughan, then on to Lisdoonvarna, coachloads of tourists pass at intervals, heading pellmell for the Cliffs of Moher, but beyond that the area is desolate, deserted, and in all weathers unutterably beautiful.

Fortunately, the travellers who appreciate the Burren do not come to this *Boireann*, this 'rocky district', for trees or water, so much as for the fantastic display of carboniferous limestone bulging out of the hills, beneath whose gryke-studded surface there is a wealth of caves.

The Burren is about twenty-five miles across from east to west, and fifteen miles from north to south, wedged between the seas of Galway Bay and the Atlantic, down as far as Doolin, just north of the Cliffs of Moher, and the inland towns of Kilfenora, Gort and Invarra. The sea is therefore never far away from the Burren, and one feels that it is the salt water's promise which keeps these grey-white rocks from entirely

shrivelling the surface of the land. As a carboniferous landscape it is a late product of the Ice Age, containing all those wonderful natural formations associated with glacial movements – clints and grykes, underground rivers and caves.

The scoring of the limestone by the dragged detritus of the ice-flows which began the formation of grykes would also suggest the presence of erratics – those heavy boulders carried in and upon the ice-flows and deposited, in a strange dislocation of space and time, when they melted. And, indeed, erratics are found almost everywhere in the Burren, although the finest examples are those which balance on the limestone slopes of clints, down at the sea edge on

Above: The undulating white limestone of the Burren, which appears to shimmer silver in the sunlight.

Above right: The long grykes of the Burren pavements of limestone. Some of these are as much as fifteen feet deep.

Right: The whole area of the Burren is littered with boulders and erratics. Beyond this boulder is the ancient man-made Poulnabrone monument.

Black Head, jutting into Galway Bay. These erratics, which are anything from five to seven feet high, are often split into exotic sculptural forms by ice-cracks and erosion, and stand proudly on or near the limestone pavements which front directly onto the waves.

Slieve Elva, with its 1,134 feet, is the highest of the hills in the Burren, but it is not its size which impresses so much as its grey-white dazzle, the soft textures of its treeless stone undulation, and all the man-made adornments on its surface and on the surrounding hills. All around dry-stone walls, ancient forts, grave-yards, ruined churches, castles and ancient cromlech burials lie scattered, stone upon stone, in this lunar earth. TD Robinson, who drew up a map of the Burren, rightly says that the area could be defined by its rich concentration of archaeological sites alone. In support of this idea, he counted some 450 ring-forts in this relatively small stretch of karst.

Clints and grykes are everywhere, burrowed deep into the limestone: they are the distinctive patina of the Burren. On the whole, the grykes are fairly narrow, only rarely above a foot or so wide, but they can drop as much as 20 feet. The finest ones are those on either side of the aptly named Corkscrew Hill. Long chains of grykes, looking for all the world like the savage cleft of a gigantic axe-head in the rocks, stretch up to fifty or sixty feet in length; some of these can be most conveniently seen in the fields which contain the two best preserved of these wedge-shaped graves, whose stone roofs tilt to the west and taper to the east. The finest of these is the Poulnabrone, with a thirteen-foot capstone, five miles south-west of Ballyvaughan.

Late spring is the most beautiful time in this curious land, when its barrenness is cast off and it becomes fertile in colours. White or pale pink hawthorn in the valley hedges, gentian and spiked orchid, yellow Mountain Avens, the red flowers of the bee-orchid, which imitates the form of the insect after which it is named, the

bell-shaped anemone stripe of the creeping *calystegia soldanella*, the white corkscrew of Lady's Tresses, and the stunning purples of the insectivorous Greater Butterwort, all burst forth as splashes of hue against the omnipresent greys and white of the limestone.

Like most limestone regions, the Burren is honeycombed with cave systems, especially the areas below Slieve Elva and Poulacapple, the finest of which is the seven-and-a-half-mile system of Pollnagollum on the north-eastern slopes of the Slieve, with a vertical shaft of 1,000 feet. Aillwee Cave is the only show-cave of the Burren, first discovered in 1944 and opened to the public in 1976. The stalagmites and stalactites grouped within the cave, mainly along the walls, are alone well worth a visit, but there is also one large striated blanket, hopelessly misnamed the 'pig's ear' in the cavern roof of Mud Hall, which has fine examples of straw stalactites in both main chambers. Most impressive, however, among all these is the fact that boulders of the granite from Connemara have been carried by the ice flows across the lands now covered by the seas of Galway Bay – perhaps among the most remarkable of all erratics, left not as a startling deposit on top of a limestone socle, but deeply immersed below this uncompromising surface of stone hills.

Left: One of the snow-flow walls of the Aillwee Cave in the Burren, the only show-cave in an area which is, in fact, riddled with cave systems.

Below: One of the lovely erratics of the Burren. The finest of these are found dotting the landscape above Black Head which encloses part of Galway Bay.

The central cliff in the Moher range, topped by O'Brien's Tower. The massive horizontal rock shelves are quite natural.

Cliffs of Moher

The cliffs of Moher ... so sheer and inhospitable that even the sea birds seem to have despaired of finding any shelter for nesting. In misty weather they look even more enormous, like the nightmare of some deranged god; in fine weather, particularly at sunset, they belong to mythology and the underworld.
James Plunkett

'... the imperturbable contemptuous Cliffs of Moher', Kate O'Brien calls them in her book, *My Ireland*, and, as so often with the Irish pen, the words are right and absolute. Yet, for all their disdain of man, these cliffs are the most popular of seaward precipices in Ireland. They rear up vertically, as though petrified in astonishment at the vociferous waves, a display of sheer dark sandstones, with a distinctive jagged band of red sandstone stratifications below the dark shale near the top. These characteristic strata jut out from the cliff face in a series of long horizontal bands, ripped into jagged teeth by the ages, and the shale and soil at the top sufficiently flattened out to allow the visitor to walk safely upon the sandstone ridge, so as to view and experience the dizzy drop into the Atlantic below.

The highest stretch of the Moher cliffs is at the northern end, where they rise some 668 feet above the waves. The cliffs at the southern end are not so impressive, for all their 400 feet, yet it is this stretch which gave the entire five miles of precipice its name. Moher is from the ancient Gaelic *Mothair*, which was the name given to the ancient cliff fort which spread over Hag's Head to the south: this fort, or rather the remains of it, were desecrated in the last century to make place for the uninteresting signals tower which still remains although it was not in use for long.

Understandably, it is towards the northern end that the tourists are directed from the car park along well-worn pathways where they are protected from winds and the larger amounts of windblown spray by enormous flagstones. They are channelled by these pathways to O'Brien's Tower, which was erected in 1835 as a 'gothic castle' tea-house. The pity is that these pathways do not lead directly to the most stupendous views offered by the cliffs.

The finest panoramic view is that to be had by continuing north beyond O'Brien's Tower to the extreme end of the cliffs. From here there is a clear prospect of the 220-foot-high sea-stack below the Tower and an unimpeded view of the layers of red sandstone which zig-zag along the upper edges of the northern face.

In fact the most extraordinary views of the cliffs are not to be had from the top at all, but from the rocky shore below the northern cliffs. This might, of course, sensibly argue for the hire of a boat from nearby Liscannor, but it is possible for the foolhardy or courageous to climb down the innocent-seeming greensward cliffs to the extreme north of the Moher. The fact that this pathway peters out as the going becomes almost vertical, argues that many start the climb, but few finish. One hopes that those who do not continue turn back! This climb is indeed far from easy, especially at the bottom, but is well worth the risks, for the full splendour of the northern face is revealed and is seen not as a mere vertical defiance of the Atlantic but as an over-beetling cliff, ready, as it seems from below, to crash down and add yet more boulders to this devastated seashore. Indeed, perhaps the most surprising thing revealed by this climb is that what was seen from above as a fine shingle beach is, in fact, littered with enormous, smooth and colourful boulders, many of them as high as a man, so do the distances distort.

Right: The sea-stack below O'Brien's Tower, seen from the boulder-littered shore.

Middle right: A three-mile stretch of cliffs, ranging south towards Loop Head, itself not visible.

Far right: Sunset over the Aran Islands, seen from one of the ledges in the northern range of the Moher cliffs.

It is quite possible to clamber across and over these rocks southwards, along the bottom of the cliff, until you reach the cliffs below O'Brien's Tower, although it is very important to be careful of the tides, which can cut you off. From here you get the finest views of the sea-stack and hear the crash of waves which from above appear to move so silently and slowly.

Guidebooks tell of the gales carrying seaspray up the full height of the cliffs, but one can be drenched by wind-flung spray even on relatively calm days, such is the force of the elements in this extraordinary place. From above there is a deceptive silence, for the crash

of waves at the cliff base is scarcely heard, and even the distant movements and screams of birds evoke little sound.

From the top of these jagged and pointed slabs of sandstone strata one has an exquisite view of the Aran Islands, and the sunset from this vantage point is surely one of the most magical in this magical land. The nuances of russets, reds and yellows which dissolve the aqueous blues as darkness comes are so hypnotic that one becomes blind to the sheer drop below, until suddenly a sea-bird wheels up from nowhere, reminding you that below there is nothing for nigh on seven hundred feet, and then the silent crash of waves on pebbles as big as a man.

Donegal

To go to Donegal for the sake of the scenery only is to miss the most rewarding thing. Here you have an ideal civilisation, an Arcadia that is worth coming from the ends of the earth to study.

Stephen Rynne

The Derryveagh Mountains to the south of Errigal, one of the characteristic chains of Donegal.

One of the most telling aspects of Donegal is to be found in the meaning in its name, evocative of the natural splendour of a quiltwork of mountains isolated in the north-western part of an island, for *Donegal* means 'stronghold of the stranger'. It is a beautiful stronghold, kept safe and secure by highlands whose mountains, forming a lunar crescent from Slieve League through to Derryveagh Mountains, constitute at once a barrier against modern life and a protection for those fortunate enough to live within.

As you drive or walk across the heather-covered Derryveagh Mountains, you become accustomed to the browns and greens of this land, colours relieved here and there by a brilliant slash of grassland or by the black brickwork of peat-diggings. Then, quite suddenly, when you look upwards towards the mountain peak of Errigal you are dazzled, for you see the pure white snow reflecting a silver sheen. This later proves not to be snow but quartzite which flakes in screes down from the sharp sides of the peak. However, the exact nature of the relieving whiteness is unimportant against the shock and its mysterious beauty. 'Perhaps', writes the author Pochin Mould, 'it is the most striking of the Irish peaks, a sudden white pyramid of quartzite springing up solitary from the plain.'

Errigal is 2,466 feet high, with a name which some have linked with eagles, but which is apparently from *Airecal Adhamhnain*, meaning 'the oratory of St Adamnan', the saint being the biographer of St Columcille; perhaps there was at one time an important church in this area. The real allurement of Errigal, however, is the contrast it affords with the other mountains of these regions of Donegal. You can stand before Errigal a mile west of Dunlewy and contrast this sharp white peak with the nobbed, curled and rounded range of the Derryveaghs to the south, especially of Slieve Snacht, the 'mountains of snow' as the original Gaelic has it, the peaks of

which show the characteristic signs of ice-smoothing. Incredible as it may seem, there is evidence that the ices of the glacial periods covered mighty Errigal, with sheets at least 2,500 feet thick, and it was the retreat of such packs which rounded off the mountains to the south. It is the extraordinary variety of the Donegal mountains which gives them their reputation. The contrast, for instance, between the sharp tor of white Errigal and the smooth plateau of the blue Muckish only a few miles distant is one worth observing. The form of the Muckish gives away the secret of its curious name, which is almost humorous to English

Above: The white scree-strewn peak of Errigal contrasts strongly with the dark rocks of the Donegal mountains.

Right: The Muckish range with its characteristic 'pig's back' lies to the east of Errigal.

ears, yet quite pedestrian for the Irish. *Muc Ais*, the original Gaelic, simply means 'pig's back', and one scarcely needs to be fanciful to trace in the distinctive silhouette of this plateau-like mountain the heavy back of a well-fed hog.

If you drive through the road gap at Dunlewy, which lies between Errigal and the Derryveaghs, and continue east towards Letterkenny, within less than four miles you are rewarded by an unrivalled view of the Muckish range behind you to the south. Such a drive or walk is advised, even for those passing through Donegal in a hurry, for it will present the finest unscaled views of the three main mountain gems of this wonderful country. A little more effort is required for the pass in the Glendowan Mountains, which is reached by way of the road alongside Garten Lough, north-west of Letterkenny. From this pass you can have breathtaking views of Donegal, with Slieve Snacht, at some 2,240 feet, to the south-west, and Dooish, at 2,147 feet, to the north.

The glens within the Derryveagh Mountains are especially possessed of a wild beauty, with trees recalling the Gaelic origin of the name – *Doire bheathach*, 'birch wood'. Perhaps the Poisoned Glen is the most impressive, settled within the enclosing mountains, the head forming an enormous amphitheatre. This glen is

almost as misnamed as 'Bloody Foreland' to the north of Donegal, which suggests awful shipwrecks but which in reality indicates red sunsets, for it is not itself poisonous, although the spurge *Euphorbia* grows in it and is reputed to make the waters of the glen poisonous to humans. To the north-east is Glenveagh Deer Forest, to the south the cliff-edged Gap of Ballaghgeeha, both places of great beauty themselves.

The glen Glencolumbkille has a name which proclaims its most cherished building – the church associated with St Columcille – with perhaps more accuracy than the many stories attached to the saint himself. It is an oratory, or small chapel, rather than a church, although it was once the site of his monastery. The flagstone to the south, above Lough Gartan, may well be the stone upon which the saint was born, but a cold coming he would have had, and I question the popular notion that anyone who sleeps upon this stone will be cured of homesickness. How, in any case, can you be homesick amidst such beauty as is offered by the mountains of Donegal? Mountains can often seem hostile – splendid yet inhuman – but among the rocks of Donegal I feel only a sense of welcome, of being no stranger.

Giant's Causeway

... not only as Remarkable a Natural Curiosity of its sort as this Country affords, but perhaps as may be met with in Europe.

Sir Thomas Molyneux

Thus Thomas Molyneux praised the Giant's Causeway on the north coast of Ireland, when he sent the first artist to make careful drawings of it, as early as 1697. This was, of course, long before the next century 'discovered' the similar basaltic formations on the island of Staffa, off Scotland.

Just as with Staffa, these basaltic pavements of the Giant's Causeway were seen as the work of giants, or as an example of the 'art' of nature. 'The famed wonder of the North', Sir Richard Hoare called the Causeway; 'one of the world's strangest phenomena', insist Newly and Petry in their modern guidebook, and all the records mention the legends which ascribe the building of the pavements to giants. Some say they were intended as the landing place for the ancient giants who waded across the seas, while others insist that they mark the remnant of a causeway which once spanned the Irish Sea as far as Scotland, the work of the legendary Finn Mac-Coul who wished to make the crossing without wetting his feet. However, the Causeway itself would make uncomfortable walking, even for giants, as it is made up of undulating basaltic patchwork quilts of regular and irregular polygonal columns, unevenly set, which disappear into the sea northwards, as though indeed reaching out to the Hebrides.

When the theory of 'giant constructors' was rejected by the early geologists, the pavements were seen as the handicraft of nature, who was herself an artist. The antiquary, William Hamilton, who was murdered for his support of the British government, and after whom the 'seat' on Pleaskin Head (one of the substantial headlands east of the Causeway) is named, wrote at length about the 'natural architecture' of the basalts, thus setting the scene for the more contentious writings of Ruskin, who saw such phenomena as the result of 'Divine Counsels'. Whether nature made the giants, who then built the pavements, or whether nature herself sculpted them, may be quite irrelevant in the

face of the no less romantic visions afforded us by modern geologists, whose giant constructors are the magmatic furies within the earth, which periodically escape through volcanic activity.

These displays of basalt around and upon the Giant's Causeway are the result of widespread volcanic activity which took place about 60 million years ago. The Antrim plateau is the largest remaining display of such activity in the entire British Isles, and can be seen quite clearly, even to this day, to have been the result of a steady flow of lava from earth fissures. The group of basaltic formations which are of immediate interest to us here are the well-formed polygonal structures which are found within the Causeway and on the higher outcroppings

Above: The hexagonal basalts of the Giant's Causeway with Port Noffer beyond.

Right: The vertical columns of the most westerly of the basalt peninsulas.

117

Right: The tilt of the hexagonal basaltic columns is very pronounced in some parts of the three peninsulas. This area slopes up to the crown of the most easterly peninsula.

Below right: Two huge boulders on the shore at Port Noffer, with a natural sea-stack beyond.

segmented horizontally, resulting in what has been called 'the ball and socket' system, with columns carried within columns, as is evident within the Giant's Organ.

Most of the columns nestle together in verticals, though some tilt at 30° to the vertical. The outcroppings of the Causeway itself extend some two hundred yards out to sea in a series of pentagonal steps ranging down from a height of about thirty-five feet, until they finally merge with the waves and then plunge below them. It is estimated that there are some 32,000 such columns, intricately fitted together.

The plethora of stories and the many fanciful

Above: The long hexagonal verticals of the so-called Giant's Organ.

Right: A section of the innermost peninsula painted red by the late evening sunlight.

in what is called 'The Giant's Organ' – these are distinguished by geologists as the 'middle basalts' or 'interbasalts'. The Causeway is in fact a trident-shaped outcropping of formations, reaching into the sea between two headlands of the Antrim coast, which is itself scattered with quite extraordinary basalts. Geological research has shown that, in theory at least, the cooling process which followed on the exudation of basalts from the interior of the earth should produce a regular polygonal network of columns, yet there are to be found on the Causeway a large number of pentagonal structures, and indeed, four, seven, eight, nine and even ten-sided columns. Another characteristic of the cooling process is that many of the columns are

names ascribed to the basaltic formations on and around the Causeway were invented for tourists. None of the names is of great antiquity, for they can all be traced to the beginnings of the tourist industry in the early nineteenth century. The names, once listed, say it all: we have the Giant's Wishing Chair, the Giant's Grandmother, the Giant's Gate, the Giant's Organ, the Fan, the Mitre, and so on.

The famous Giant's Wishing Chair is made up of a low-set series of hexagonal columns within a semi-circle of six raised columns which form the back rest to the 'chair'. It is possible that the Giant's Gate was made by people to allow an easy passage through towards Hamilton's Seat and Port Noffer, to the east.

Giant's Causeway itself, the most lovely of the basalt formations, is divided into three main peninsulas, which, ranging from west to east, are known as the Little Causeway, the Middle Causeway (sometimes called the Honeycomb), and the Grand Causeway. Without doubt, it is from the Grand Causeway that one sees to advantage the magical work of the ancient basalts. It is possible to stand here with perfect hexagonal columns at one's feet, and see the distinctive interbasaltic beds framed by the eastern headland around Port Noffer (originally *port an Aifir*, 'the giant's port') whose weathered

basaltic outcroppings tower above them. The rich reds of the soil layers are iron oxides and alumina, while the grey-greens are rich in silica, containing also the curiosity known as 'giant's eyes', which are in fact kernels of black basalt.

Eastward and westward from the National Trust car park at the entrance to the Causeway there are breathtaking walks and natural curiosities which are less famous only because they are dwarfed by their proximity to this magnificent formation. The caves of Portcoon and Runkerry to the east are well worth a visit, and their splendour and size would have made them special wonders in any other setting than these myth-strewn basalts, while the ten miles of cliff-walks westwards along Causeway Head to Bengore Head, by way of the Organ, the Chimney Tops and Hamilton's Seat are also well worth the labour and the inevitable battle against the winds. The finest walk is actually along the rock-littered cliff base immediately contiguous with the Causeways, following the coastal path up and around the interbasaltic beds around Port Noffer until it joins the top of the cliffs.

The splendid variety of these basalts, most of them built from the mysterious hexagonals, proclaim this short stretch of coastline the supreme natural wonder of Ireland.

Below: The central peninsula of the Causeways (here seen from the west) would be an uncomfortable landing-stage, even for a giant.

Left: Rock forms twisted into strange sculptural forms by intense heat, millions of years ago. This formation lies to the south of the westerly path to the Causeways.

Killarney

In the morning when I awoke and saw the mountains and the breathing waters and the little islands below me, miles away, all slowly emerging from their mists with the clarity of a dream from sleep, I knew that I was seeing the real Killarney.

Sean O'Faolain

The lakes of Killarney from Ladies' View, which offers a splendid panorama of the area below the southern mountains of Killarney.

Almost any seasoned traveller you meet in Ireland will tell you that Killarney is the most beautiful part of this land, but none of them will have in mind the town itself. Killarney, they know, has been destroyed by tourism, and is perhaps the only blot on this exquisitely varied part of Ireland. To prove their point, such travellers will direct you impatiently away from the town, to the south or to the west, where, within a few miles' compass, there are three outstanding natural wonders of Ireland set within a land of mountains and lakes which are wonders in themselves. The traveller will invite you to see a gap in the mountains, a viewpoint halfway up a mountain, and the highest mountain in Ireland. He will make no mention of lakes, for every traveller takes it for granted that you already know that the lakes of Killarney are like no other lakes you will ever see.

The gap through the mountains is the Gap of Dunloe, which has a unique romanticism which makes it an Irish attraction that must not be missed: you have to visit this mountain gap early in the morning, or late at night, in order to avoid the tourists and the hordes of donkey carts which serve them. The second of the Killarney wonders is perhaps the most famous viewpoint in Ireland, snuggled into a roadside which skirts the descent of Macgillicuddy's Reeks, and called 'Ladies' View'. From here, the lakes are at your feet, and the blue ring of mountains spread themselves around in great laziness and beauty, in open proclamation that time in Ireland is different from time in any other land. From this viewpoint you will see in the distance the third of the Killarney wonders – the highest mountain in Ireland and crown of Macgillicuddy's Reeks, Carrantoul, usually pushing mists upwards to hide its peak of 3,414 feet. The name, sometimes Carrantuohill in modern spelling, is from the Gaelic *Corran Tuathail*, which is usually translated as meaning 'inverted reaping hook'.

To arrive at any of these three places, you

Above: The lower lake of Killarney, to the south of the town itself.

must walk or drive through the lake-riddled hills of Killarney – hills which are as S P B Mais admits, 'grand, majestic, intimidating and quite lovely – worth crossing the world to see'.

There are three main lakes near Killarney. The Lower Lake is by far the largest and is separated from the Middle Lake by the peninsula of Muckross. This Middle Lake is bound to the Upper Lake by an umbilical cord-like strait called the Long Range. Around all three are swathes of luxuriant forest, sheltering ferns, mosses and liverworts and behind are the mountain ranges. The limestone of the Lower Lake has been sculpted by erosion into fascinating shapes, and is still fed by waterfalls.

The Gap of Dunloe is some six miles southwest of Killarney. It is now an unsurfaced but just usable track-road which winds up, around and between high mountain ranges: on all sides of the road there are crags and mountains, green grasses, ferns and mosses spattered with boulders which from the distance look small enough to trip over, but which on approach are found to be almost too large to be climbed. Macgillicuddy's Reeks form the most impressive of the steep walls which threaten the gap to the west, dominated by Carrantoul which is faced by the Purple Mountain, at 2,739 feet, and the slightly lower Tomies to the east.

The road wrestles its way through these frighteningly beautiful mountains, like a faltering switchback through the ice-gouged gap, sometimes almost over into, but always never far from, the *loughs* of peat-black waters, ominous in dark and overcast weather, sparkling with joy in the sun, and turned to a hellfire red in the sunset.

Legend tells us that St Patrick drowned the last Irish snake in one of these loughs, set like pieces of sky among the stones. The event should perhaps be read symbolically – the snake was of course the 'old serpent', the devil, with whom St Patrick wrestled, and after the work of the saint Ireland was seen as free from the ravages of the devil.

In places Dunloe Gap is strikingly beautiful, but it is also capable of inducing a shudder, as though the place has some awful memory, which even the years of tourism have not yet washed clean. For those who know the Gap from engravings and paintings first sight can be disappointing. The rocks are not as large, the fall of the hills not as steep and the crags not as savage, as artists have shown them. Yet after only a few hours wandering in the Gap, one can see why artists have felt the need to exaggerate the forms – they could not express the wild intensity of the place without distorting its physical appearance, for its spirit is stronger than the mere external forms of rocks, stones and water.

The switchback road delights in destroying car springs, as though it were a dragon with a hatred of mechanical things, and only a well-armoured car will negotiate the pass. And yet, if you drive, you will miss the real beauty of Dunloe, which calls for a meditative walk, and for all those timeless recollections of tranquillity which are the hallmarks of the romantic experience towards which Dunloe and its surroundings beckon us.

Below: The Gap of Dunloe, looking south, with Macgillicuddy's Reeks to the west.

Loop Head

The lighthouse of Loop Head ... is the exile's last glimpse of Erin ...

Kate O'Brien

The cliffs of Loop Head are not half the height of those further north at Moher, yet they are more varied, more tortuous in form, and have the advantage of two magnificent natural formations. A vast and crudely severed extension of the Head, just beyond the lighthouse, is now called 'Dermot and Grania's Rock', a point famous in mythology and history. In mythology it evokes the great hero Cuchullainn, sometimes called the Hercules of Celtic mythology. A 'footprint', said to be that of Cuchullainn, is to be seen on the landward side of the chasm at the end of the Loop, a print left when he leapt this chasm to escape the attention of a woman who pursued him. The story of Cuchullainn, who would kill a hundred men a day with his sling, is, as James Plunkett wickedly observes, yet another saga of the unending trouble that Irish saints and heroes, both pagan and Christian, seem to have had with women! In history, the Loop draws its fame from one sad fact, for the lighthouse at its tip 'is the exile's last glimpse of Erin'.

The most magnificent of the Loop Head formations appears to bear no special name: it is a wonderful sea-arch at the end of a long and sheer cliff, about half a mile east of the lighthouse, a sixty-foot slash into a promontory which dazzles the eyes with its stretch of white stratifications. There is a knife-edged, grass-covered juncture to the headland which juts seawards to the west of this sea-arch, and the balancing act required to cross the junction is rewarded with the finest view of the stratified cliffs which terminate in this arch. The scream of the gulls and other sea-birds which infest this narrow and dangerous inlet add romantic poignancy to the scene, their flight appearing slow and lugubrious against the distant backcloth of black and white striations.

In the half-mile stretch of cliffs between the northern sea-arch promontory and the lighthouse, the horizontal strata change, galvanized into extraordinary convolutions. At the sea-arch

The enormous sea-arch set in the cliffs on the northern side of Loop Head.

127

promontory, the strata are as regular and horizontal as those in the amphitheatre at the Bridge of Ross, but a few hundred yards west and the stratification does a turn in upon itself, crashing down vertically in a dive which dizzily reminds one of the story that Cuchullainn was so agile that he could turn around in his own skin.

And yet, this violence takes place on the cliff precipices alone. Walking the few miles of the Loop, over a wonderful plateau of grasslands, deserted, denuded almost of trees, and virtually featureless were it not for the peat-bogs, it is possible to be so absorbed by its silent beauty that one remains totally unaware of the violent onslaught which is clearly recorded in the cliff-faces.

The snippets of history attached to the Loop are almost as violent as its myths of greatness and perfidy. At Moneen, towards the end of the peninsula, is a chapel which contains the 'bathing-machine chapel' – called the Little Ark – which was constructed for a cunning priest who was forbidden to celebrate mass during some of the worst of the Protestant excesses in Ireland. This priest, a Father Meehan, had the Ark drawn up between the watermarks on the shore of Kilbaha, beyond the authority of the English, and here for some five years around the time of

Right above: The lighthouse, which warns shipping of these dangerous cliffs, was often the last point seen by Irish emigrants.

Left: Loop head, looking west.

Right below: The northern face of the Loop peninsula, looking back towards the mainland of Ireland.

the Famine, up to 1857, he celebrated mass for a starving populace who were being offered soup by the Protestants at the price of their own religion. Such a story recalls the words of the Irishman Stephen Rynne, who insisted that 'a man who writes a book on his native country is unhappy ever after', because my feeling is that an Englishman who writes a book on Ireland must be ashamed for ever after.

The town of Kilkee is also on the Loop, and while the most activity you are likely to see there nowadays is that of the locals playing space-invaders, the Antarctic explorer, Shackleton, started his dreams here, on the yellow crescent of the reef-protected beach. Further down the Loop is Bishop's Island, now said to be inaccessible, with the remains of a hermitage dedicated to St Senan. To the west are the stratifications of shale in the Amphitheatre, and the outcrop of the Duggerna Rocks, all really a continuation of the ravaging action of the Atlantic as it moulds the sides of the Loop. This peninsula at the mouth of the River Shannon, once the place of an ancient legend, and once awash with the wreckage of the Spanish Armada, also bears the doleful distinction of being the last sight of Ireland for many thousands who left in tears to build another world on the other side of the earth.

Rock Close, Blarney

Many of the Rock Close possessions have been by tradition and in folklore associated with witchcraft and magic.
Official Guide to Blarney Castle

The natural beauties of Ireland encourage a natural eloquence, which is probably why seasoned travellers feel no need to kiss the Blarney Stone. In any case, no historian can believe in the supposed efficacy of that awkwardly placed stone: it is surely pure Blarney which encourages tourists to those unnatural gymnastics to kiss cold stone. Irish whimsicality has it that this four-foot-long stone was brought to Ireland from the Holy Land by the crusaders, who themselves believed that it was used by Jacob as his pillow. The miracle would indeed have been such a piece of Irish limestone in the Holy Land! The real history is better documented, fortunately. The word Blarney in the sense of persuasive speech was first used by, of all people, Queen Elizabeth I, who applied it to McCarthy, the Baron of the castle, whose words she had learned to distrust. The notion of the eloquence of the Blarney Stone is thus no older than the sixteenth century, and the tradition of kissing the Blarney Stone is even younger, being little over a hundred years old.

I prefer to write and think of other stones when I picture Blarney Castle. If you can tear yourself away from this rock-based tower, then you will find to the west a thick wall pierced by a narrow passageway which resembles a conduit more than a corridor. Beyond is a gentle wonderland of old trees, and even older rocks, far more eloquent than the one which is stuck a hundred or so feet up in the castle wall.

Few of these stones are very large – the biggest rocks are only between ten and fourteen feet high – but their shapes and setting are superb. On the edge of the glade, which has been offputtingly called a 'fairy dancing green', is a natural figurine which could easily be confused with a sculpture by Henry Moore, as can many of the rocks and stones here. The most lovely rock formations are to be found on every side, whether convolutions, twisted into natural portholes, on the ledge at the top of the so-called 'wishing stairs', or the imposing

Rock Close, a perfect harmony of stones and trees. While all the formations in this picture are without doubt natural, some of the boulders in other parts of the Close are the result of judicious landscaping.

131

Above: A convoluted rock which calls to mind the sculpture of Henry Moore.

Right: Stones said to be part of a Druid circle, although there is absolutely no evidence for this.

Above: A natural porthole in a rock frames the upper approach to the so-called 'wishing stairs'.

Above right: A curiously shaped standing-stone is magically transformed by shafts of sunlight.

weathered forms alongside the meandering pathway to the natural stone circle.

Much of the power of these stones lies not merely in their forms but in what the light does with them. The area is well shaded by trees, many of them extremely ancient, and through them sparking shafts of sunlight are parsimoniously thrown to the ground and upon the green lichen of the stones. When these shafts strike the inert matter a special alchemy takes place, and the dark stones are quickened to life in subtle greens, yellows and browns.

These stones also have suffered from Blarney. With all the seriousness that they can muster the guidebooks say that they are 'Druid' stones, that some of them are part of witches sabbaths, and so on. The kind of names attached to them will set the scene, no doubt; in addition to the 'wishing stairs', and 'fairy dancing green' are a 'witches' kitchen', and even a 'sacrificial altar'. It is claimed indeed that some of the upright stones are part of an ancient stone circle, but there are hundreds of stone circles throughout Ireland and Great Britain, and none are like these. They are simply rocks and stones – magical things, just as all earthly objects are magical, no more and no less.

Rock Close, to the extent that it was 'built' at all, was probably cleared and turned into a romantic attraction in the eighteenth century by James Jefferyes, who then owned the Castle. A large flat stone above the 'wishing stairs' (which are certainly man-made) is inscribed with his name and the date, 1795, but this could be merely a modern invention. But even though there probably was a certain amount of land-scaping in the eighteenth century, all the forms of these curious stones are certainly natural.

Just as wonderful as the stones are the trees. There is an ancient yew here, over a thousand years old, and an ilex tree set among flowers. There is also an ancient Cedar of Lebanon in the Close which came all the way from the Holy Land, and perhaps it was this which the scribes confused with the stone of Blarney?

Right: The last view of the sunset in the British Isles, or indeed in Europe. The Skelligs lie at the furthest western point in the British Isles.

Below: The 'snow'-touched fangs of Little Skellig, framed by a natural outcrop about a third of the way up Skellig Michael.

The Skelligs

For the monks of Skellig Michael, Heaven was above, Hell was below. The stars were lit at night by angels and quenched at dawn. The winds tearing at the rock and the seas when they sought to devour it were moved by demons...
James Plunkett

West of Bolus Head in County Kerry, some eight miles out in the Atlantic, the sea-bed shows a pair of rock fangs looking towards the distant Americas. These are the rocks of the Skelligs, the larger being Skellig Michael and its neighbour further west the Little Skellig. Both these rocks are fantastic tips of grit and shale mountains, veined with quartz within, and covered on the outside with an undulating coat of sea-birds. They are now uninhabited, save for a lighthouse keeper who keeps uneasy vigil on Skellig Michael, as aware of the demons tearing and devouring as were monks who lived on the rock long ago.

The Little Skellig is the home of gannets, called the 'mad ones' by the French because of the insanity of their vertical dive into the sea spume in search of fish. The white of their bodies and the slow flurry of their sailing flight give the Little Skellig all the appearance from a distance of being covered in snow. The occasional gannet is also seen on Skellig Michael, but more frequent on this larger rock are stormy petrels, fulmars – so touchingly curious about humans – gulls and puffins, who appear to be quite unafraid of man.

The curious name, *Skellig*, is from the old Irish and means 'gleaming', perhaps referring to the gleams of light which are reflected from the rocks in bright sunshine – an effect best seen from Bolus Head. The name Michael is probably of monastic origin, reminiscent of the old Christian tradition of establishing monasteries in high places.

Skellig Michael is ominous and sheer, its forty or so acres of rock culminating in two peaks, the highest of which is 715 feet above the seas, although the ambitious leap of the waves is often sufficient to reduce this by a hundred feet or more. Waves will even lick the windows of the lighthouse, which is more than halfway up the rock.

The main peak is a rock chimney called 'the Eye of the Needle', suggesting that at one time there was a wind-hole through the summit which has long since fallen away; traces of such are visible from the saddle of rock which joins the two peaks. Right up until this century the Eye was the object of an incredible feat of pilgrimage, involving a dangerous climb to kiss a cross at the top. In the not too distant past there had been a slight, body-twisting and entirely dangerous corkscrew pathway, ending in a twelve-foot rock which could be negotiated by means of foot-holes and hand-grips, leading to a projection upon which the cross was embedded. However, a recent cliff-collapse has obliterated the path, so now rope and tackle, as much as insane courage, are required to kiss the cross.

The other peak, almost as high at 650 feet, is more easily scaled because of the industry of the early monks who laboriously heaved into place a stone stairway of 558 steps. That is the number of these enormous steps at the present time, although as the climb now starts at a higher level than the monks' original landing point had access to, it is possible that at one time there might well have been nearer a thousand steps to make up this back-breaking climb to the summit.

Whatever their number, these steps lead to what is probably the earliest of surviving monastic centres in Europe, for nestling into the protective mass of the northern peaks are seventh-century remains associated with the monks of St Finan (or Fionan). There is a ruined church here, five natural wells and seven corbel-roofed beehive-shaped stone huts known as *clochans*, along with two burial areas and a number of gardens, the entire complex being hedged in by a series of massive dry-stone walls. The gardens are now wild, but lovely, and testimony to an extraordinary devotion, for the rock of Skellig offered little earth for growth, and it is assumed that the monks painstakingly collected such earth as they could find in the crevices of their chosen rock, and packed it,

135

handful by handful, to make the gardens in which they might grow food.

This early settlement was raided by the Vikings in 823 and finally deserted by the monks for the mainland in 1044, after the main work of converting Europe, which had been the chosen destiny of the Irish monks, had been completed. Altogether they appear to have lived on this isolated rock eyrie – perhaps in communities of twenty to twenty-five men – for nearly seven hundred years, and much of the intensity of their inner peace and religious devotion remains here still. This forlorn and beautiful place is one of the most poignant and spiritually charged remains in the whole of Europe.

The stone remains of the church show that it had a most interesting orientation. If one stands where the altar would have been, and where the monks would have witnessed at matins the rising of the sun (reminding us of the mediaeval manuscripts which describe the Archangel Michael as the Archangel of the Sun), by the gravestone of two children of a former lighthouse keeper, one sees, framed by the slit of the eastern window, the shape of the Little Skellig, hovering over the waves, with the expanse of the dawning red sky above. Thus, each day the monks would have been reminded of the essen-

Right: The last flight of massive stone steps, which lead up to the monastic settlement on Skellig Michael. They were built by the monks over a thousand years ago.

tial unity of things in this meeting of the four elements of fire (sun), earth (Little Skellig), water (the Atlantic seas), and air (the clouds of the sky).

Perhaps for modern man, however, it is the sunset from Skellig Michael which is the most impressive sight. If you scramble up the incline of rock behind the monastic site you will come to a razor-edged precipice which confronts America. If you manage to stay perched up there long enough – a privilege granted only to those who have permission to stay overnight on the rock – and the weather is clear, then you will experience the final splendid sunset over Europe, for this rock is the furthest point west in the continent.

SCOTLAND

PICTURE: THE OLD MAN OF HOY – SEE PAGE 172

Introduction

*Mountains open their hinged reflections on the
    loch,
And these reflections, pummelled by the wind,
Shape and reshape themselves, grow squat or
    tall,
Are bent by shakes of light. We never find
The same place twice...*

                                        Maurice Lindsay

In his fine poem about Loch Lomond, Maurice
Lindsay touches on the ancient Greek theme of
the transience of nature. Just as you can never
step into the same stream twice, for its waters
are always changing, so you can never see the
same view twice. He says that coloured post-
cards 'that claim to lay the constant on the table'
are popular, for they are a reassuring fable
offering permanence, but the images they give
are false. In this land the weather and light
conspire to demonstrate that what we might
superficially take to be 'eternal' or 'unchange-
able' – the mountains, lochs and glens – are
transiency itself. We may try to grasp at the
experience but we can never hold it.

Perhaps it is true that the effect of transience
is magnified in the lochs, which one minute
threaten and chill with darkened skies, and
then of a sudden burst out in a rainbow smile, a
moment later, to deck themselves with azures.
The sun-drenched rock on the beach of Mull
(page 143) was photographed within less than
half an hour of the sombre landscape a quarter
of a mile inland (pages 142–3). This is the
fundamental experience of Scotland. Photographs disappoint, because it is as though you
photograph the face of a friend, and find on the
negative the image of someone you do not
know. These eternal mountains, hills and glens
will not stay in place, will not be captured.

And yet, the sight of the natural wonders of
Scotland is enriching and does offer a sort of
permanence to the soul. The geologist Faujas de
Saint Fond, who in 1784 travelled via Loch
Lomond to make the first serious scientific
studies of the island of Staffa, eulogized upon
the Loch, but also pointed to how it works itself
into our being. 'The superb Loch Lomond,' he
writes, 'the fine sunlight that gilded its waters,
the silvery rocks that skirted its shores, the
flowery and verdant mosses, the black oxen, the
white sheep, the shepherds beneath the pines
... will never be effaced from my memory, and
make me cherish the desire not to die before

Right: Ben Nevis in a rainstorm, relieved by unexpected rays of sunlight.

Below left: Bass Island, seen from the walls of Tantallon Castle.

again seeing Tarbet. I shall often dream of Tarbet, even in the midst of lovely Italy with its oranges, its myrtles, its laurels, and its jessamines.'

Saint Fond is right, for Scotland lives powerfully in the soul, colouring sleep with pleasant dreams, enriching the waking day with memory. There is an element of unreality to this land. After visiting the sites of the wonders, perhaps even living with them or near them for some days, I turn away and find myself wondering if I had really been there. So deeply have I experienced this dream-like quality that I have been delighted to find other writers and poets echo my experience. Perhaps this is the reason why Scotsmen travel: the essence of Scotland

Above: Loch Leven, looking north – one of the great beauties of Scotland.

141

There are so many astounding sea-stacks in Scotland, the choice was almost embarrassing. Of course, the Old Man of Hoy beckons imperiously, but he is closely challenged by the Stack of Handa and by the Old Man of Stoer, and quite out-spired by the Stac Lee on St Kilda's, with its height of 544 feet, described by Sir Julian Huxley as 'the most majestic sea-rock in existence'. The stack at Yesnaby is included because of its distinctive shape, the stacks at Duncansby because they remind me of a battlefield after a mighty war, and stand witness to the destructive power of natural forces.

I have allowed my fancy free rein in the choice of Scottish rocks. First I chose the extremes of the 'largest' and the 'smallest' in the Cairngorms and the Dunnottar Fiddlehead. The Cairngorms form the largest massif in Great Britain, a plateau of mountains which even in this technological age has left huge stretches of Scottish cartography without a road. The smallest stones are the richly veined pebbles in the Fiddlehead conglomerates, which ironically enough might have been formed from the weathered fragments of rocks made at the same time that the Cairngorm massif was raised. Had this book been dealing with other things than natural wonders, then Dunnottar might well have been chosen for its castle alone, the finest

cannot be grasped within the country itself, but can be carried with impunity in the memory.

The dreams which have been reduced to coloured photographs and words are very special ones, of course. In most cases there was little choosing, for the wonders had an imperative voice of their own. Staffa had to be included. It has a romanticism of its own. There are times when I feel that perhaps it did not lie unnoticed (or rather unsung) until the eighteenth century in order to be discovered by Romantic writers, as is generally believed – perhaps it emerged into the world in order to help create Romanticism itself!

Scotland must also have its representative glen, and this can only be Glencoe. There are other points of view: some would claim that Glencoe is no great beauty, and would place before it the Glen of Afric, or perhaps Glen Lyon. Yet its attraction lies in its wildness, with which no other glen I know can complete. As W H Murray says, in his book, *The West Highlands of Scotland*, the glen is 'of its own kind unrivalled. All other glens seem tame by comparison: they are certainly not so uncompromisingly precipitous.' The loch must be Loch Lomond. A whole book of eulogies on this loch might well be published, for it is one that has caused almost universal delight.

of its kind in this land. Only comparable is the extraordinary Tantallon, with its Bass Rock hanging alongside, which would deserve a place in any longer book of natural wonders.

The choice of the rocks of Mull is entirely personal. I delight in those rocks which promise the 'eternal' and are sublime in the sunlight. I also delight unashamedly in the splendour with which the sun sets over this beautiful island. At least one other traveller, Campbell Steven, has recorded a similar transport of delight, from much the same place that I took my photographs, 'the whole sky flaming with the sunset, dazzlingly radiantly bright, and the steamer's wake making an unbroken avenue of gold into the very heart of the fire'.

The extraordinary formations at Arbroath insinuated themselves into this text because of their variety. There are other blow-holes, stacks and geos in Scotland, but there is no other place where all are gathered in such profusion and within so short a stretch.

All these wonders came easily yet there are still many others, claiming a place in the list. If any of the selection seem puzzling, then bear in mind the poem of Lindsay, and remember that the wonders in these pages are not like that, and, in any case, no one will ever be able to visit the same place twice.

Arbroath Cliffs

I should scarcely have regretted my journey had it afforded nothing more than a sight of Aberbrohoc.

Dr Johnson

Right: The fissure of Dickmont's Den, north of Arbroath.

Far right: The 'Dei'l's Head', Arbroath, at low tide.

The beautiful cliffs of Arbroath are strung out in a linear display of reds, blues and purples, although made of the so-called red sandstones, and are punctuated at intervals by quite extraordinary marine sculptures. Neither the cliffs nor these formations are of the stupendous size to which one may grow accustomed in the coastlines of Scotland: their wonder lies in the richness of colours, in the variety and delicacy of their forms, rather than in mere mass or scale.

As one walks along these cliffs the feeling grows that for once the wild North Sea has been gentle. The waves appear to have washed delicately at these rocks and coves, seeking to model rather than to sculpt with massive breakers. It is as though the sea had been intent on revealing the rich palette of colour pigments hidden within the sandstones, and the formations themselves are merely the accidental effect of this delicate work. The result is a fine quality which is altogether lacking in other places treated by the North Sea: in comparison with the cliffs of Arbroath, for example, the mangled cliffs and stacks of Duncansby, further north, have all the appearance of a battlefield.

The casual visitor is advised to follow the nature trail which has been set out with much care along the top of the Arbroath Cliffs, yet the truth is that the finest views are those to be had from the rocks and shingles of the beach itself. The going is hard along these pool-infested rocks, but a short walk along the first few hundred yards from the Arbroath side will reveal something of the beauty of the subtle purples, blues, pinks, and reds which weave themselves over the surface of the rich and ornate forms along this two-mile stretch of cliffs.

The first of the most extraordinary formations is the rock perforation called the Needle E'e, or Eye, which is an almost perfectly circular natural arch confronting the sea, like a vast porthole. There is a subtle, yet quite visible, vertical

fault through this arch, a sign to the geologist that the sea in ages past worked its way through this fault to dig out a deep sea-cave. The roof of this cave eventually collapsed, leaving the vertical wall of cliff, and its porthole door, standing serene beyond the rubble, confronting the waves, rather than lying at right angles to the beach, as do the majority of natural sea-arches. If you climb down from the cliff top towards the Needle Eye – as indeed is advisable for a perfect view of this formation – you are actually walking on the detritus of this ancient cave fall.

The Mermaid's Kirk, adjacent to it, may also be the result of a similar cave roof collapse. It is now a huge depression behind the cliff face, a steep-walled valley of sandstone, in the form of a roofless chapel. This romantic cove is inaccessible by an ordinary climb from the cliff edge, and is now scarcely touched by the sea. At full tide the waters spread limpid over its 'aisle' to leave a smooth floor of glass, only to recede again within a few minutes to leave the pebble beach enfolded within the cove like gigantic stone confetti.

However, such gentle nudgings of the waves should not lead us to imagine that these cliffs see only calms and ripples. Arbroath has its blow-hole (once more a result of a cave-fall), and when the North Sea breakers swoop into the mouth, the spray from the stormwaves leaps in that slow motion which is peculiar to spray. In times of real sea fury this spray leaps over 150

Above: The natural porthole of the 'Needle E'e'.

146

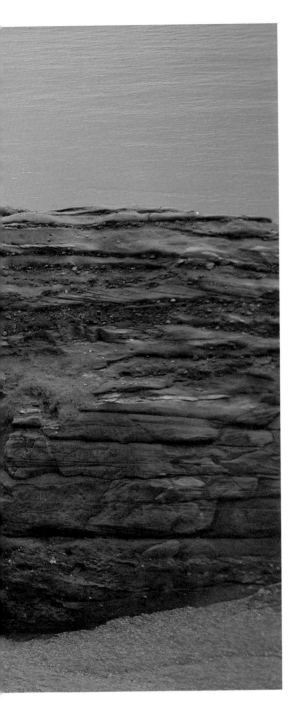

fact, a magnificent stack, perhaps seen at its best when the seas are low, revealing its contrast of dark hues against the multicoloured rock plateau which supports it. The beauty of this formation lies in the colour striations of the sandstones, in the hues of purple, red, blue and brown on the Head, in contrast to the blues and greens of its vast plinth. Were there no other geological formations along this incredible stretch of coast, De'il's Heid would surely be listed as one of the wonders of Scotland.

To the north of the Heid, beyond a man-made earthworks, are the remains of a sea-slashed headland which projects a number of rock formations further out to sea. These are named the Three Sisters, one of which is called the Camel's Back, another the Sphinx. The last name is certainly the most imaginative: any resemblance to the Sphinx must really depend on the horizontal strata of soft sandstones which are common to these formations as well as to the carved solid block near Cairo. The Three Sisters are scarcely stacks – indeed, they are probably stacks in the making – yet they do offer a most distinctive silhouette to frame Carlingheugh Bay to the north, where the pebbles on the shingle beach are superb: they look as if they had once been rainbows which shattered and fell to earth.

Below: A sea-arch to the south of De'il's Head.

feet through the circular vent, in a thrilling display which is seen chiefly in the winter.

Nearby are more varied phenomena, most of which are the results of the ancient collapsing of cave systems. The most lovely of these is the red sandstone Dickmont's Den, wedged in by the sea around a stack in the mouth of the lost cave. Here, on the cliff face above the Den, among the profusion of other flowers, orchids such as the Early Purple and the Spotted can be found – the first in spring, the second in June and July.

Beyond Dickmont's Den is a strangely wrought promontory, to the north of which stands the most famous of all the Arbroath formations, the De'il's Heid, which in spite of its name resembles no head, either human or demonic. It is, in

The Cairngorms
and Glenmore

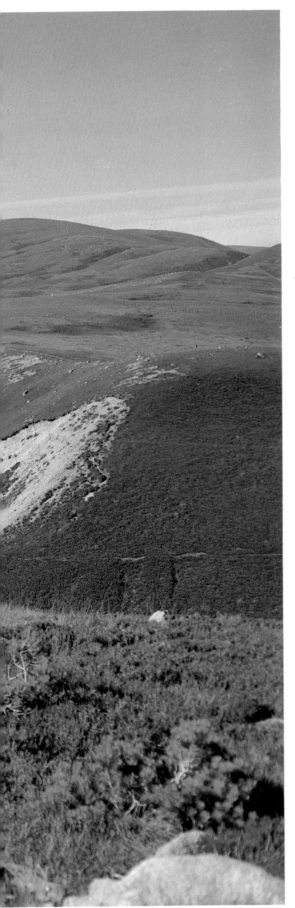

The Cairngorm Mountains ... include four of the five highest peaks in the British Isles, and by far the most extensive area over 3,000 feet ...
J G C Anderson

The Cairngorms, or 'blue hills' as they are aptly called, were once named the Monadh Ruadh, 'the red-brown hills', to differentiate them from the other Spey range, the Monadh Liath, or 'grey hills'. Both these colour names are, in fact, applicable to both ranges, for in the distance the mountains present themselves as an intense blue, while close inspection shows that the earths, marls and rocks are often red-brown, camouflaged only by the grasses, ferns and heather.

The range is granite-cored and scarred throughout with dramatic corries, but it is the range of distinctive peaks which most stir the sense of wonder in this place. The highest are those of Ben Macdui (4,296 feet), Braeriach (4,248 feet), Cairn Toul (4,241 feet), and Cairn Gorm itself (4,084 feet). In geological terminology the granite massif is part of an enormous pluton which intruded its base of some 160 square miles into the Moinian metasediments. It was during the subsequent cooling period that the quartz fragments filled the cavities, and these (with their rich range of distinctive colours) are now the famous 'cairngorm stones' which are collected in the area.

The vast plateau of peaks is remarkably isolated, for there are few roads in such wild places, and scarcely any good passes, with the result that it has retained its great beauty from ancient times. The forests, lochs and peaks remain unspoiled, bathed in a pristine freshness which speaks of the timeless. Here indeed a visitor will echo the sentiments of Sir Walter Scott, who saw among these 'crags, hills and mounds, confusedly hurl'd ... fragments of an earlier world'.

The immense plateau of mountains is pushed aside into two huge areas by the Lairig Ghru pass, which was driven inexorably through by the mighty bulldozing of the ancient glaciers, and by the Glen Dee, with its River Dee gorge. There is consequently a western group, headed by the peak of Braeriach, and an eastern group,

A stream-swept corrie on the side of Cairn Gorm, south of Glenmore.

Above: The Cairngorm range across the still morning waters of Loch Morlich.

crowned by Ben Macdui, with its Great Rough Corries, said to be the only place in Great Britain to sport a permanent snow field.

The views from the heights are prodigious, the scenery in panorama from below quite spectacular. 'It is impossible to describe the astonishment of the whole party, when they perceived themselves on the brink of that frightful precipice, which separated them from the lake below. They remained motionless for a considerable time equally struck with admiration and horror ...' Thus a traveller at the beginning of the last century writes of the experience of his party at the final ascent of the Sgoran Dubh ridge of the Cairngorms, an experience which is easily repeated today. For the less adventurous, a fine view of the Cairngorm range is to be had across the exquisite Loch Morlich in the Glenmore Forest Park, or from the heather to the west of this loch. The peaks and corries from such a vantage point include (ranging from south-east to east) Coire na Ciste, Sron an Aonaich, Cairn Gorm, rising above Coire Cas, and Coire an t-Sneachda, behind Cairn Lochan, with the distinctive peak of Creag an Letch-Choin to the south.

At the feet of these mountains, tucked away in a valley which was made fertile by glacial deposits, is the National Forest Park of Glen-more, with the single blue eye of Loch Morlich, some thousand feet above sea level, yet still slung low against the massif beyond. Loch Morlich is a water-filled kettle-hole, described in geological terms as a 'fluvio-glacial museum of outwash terraces and erratic blocks'. It is about a mile long, and two thirds of a mile broad, but by loch standards it is not very deep: what is striking about it is its beauty, and the pristine quality of its surroundings. In the forests and slopes around, the reindeer and the golden eagle (even osprey) dwell, and here also you can see the blue hare, and both red and roe deer; but most beautiful of all in Glenmore are the trees in the 3,300 acres of mainly pine and spruce. The original thick woods were pierced by the well-hidden thieves' road, the Rathad nam Mearlach, which descended by no accident on the rich cattle pastures of Banff and Moray. Many of the old Scots pine have survived, but vast tracts were destroyed mainly by man between the fifteenth and nineteenth centuries. Studies of the peat remains of such trees have shown that there was once an incredibly extensive forest stretching from Glen Lyon and Ranach to Strathspey and Strathglass, and from Glencoe eastwards to the Braes of Mar. The destruction of this forest was one of the great tragedies of Scottish history.

The Scottish love of legends and myths has peopled the Cairngorms with many curious tales and creatures. Here, for instance, is found the *each usige*, a water horse which is said to frequent especially Loch Avon, and which may be tamed only with a silver bridle. There is also the *tarb usige*, a water bull, the terrible *beithir*, a demon who lurks in caves and corries, along with the *famh*, an ugly monster who is only seen about the break of day, and on the highest verge of the mountain. His head is twice as large as his whole body.

Cairngorm stones make tiny and quite extraordinary mementoes of this massif, and may still be found in the stream-beds, slopes and corries around. They are hexagonal quartz crystals of colours varying from a smokey yellow to dark brown. Unfortunately, not all stones with such an appearance sold in local shops and tourist centres are from the Cairngorms, or even from Scotland, since a similar, though cheaper stone, is imported from Brazil.

And yet the truth is that the stripping of vast forests and the uncontrolled mining of the stones have in no significant way detracted from the gentle beauty of the lower valleys, and the isolated splendour of the higher ridges and peaks. The massif, and its nestling Glenmore Forest Park, remain serene.

Right: The trees are the greatest natural attributes of Glenmore.

Duncansby Stacks

Stand below the overwhelming grandeur of the Duncansby Stacks where natural law, careless of man's pride, has given birth to structures which rival the most formidable works of men ... And as you pass amongst the cenotaphs of forty centuries of human life, you also may feel the knowledge of your own deathless antiquity.
Farley Mowat

The popular notion that John O'Groats is the most northerly tip of the mainland should have been dispelled years ago. The truth is, of course, that the most northerly point is the magnificent Dunnet Head, some miles further to the north-west; but popular notions die slowly, if at all. John O'Groats might obtain more honest fame through its closeness to one of the most exciting coastal strips in Scotland rather than through this kind of cartographic juggling, for at nearby Duncansby the North Sea has created a monument of unsurpassed grandeur.

Caithness presents itself to the land traveller as a somewhat monotonous plateau, and so the stirring of wonderment at this eastern coastline is mingled with a sigh of relief at the sight of its confused and prolific variety of forms.

The cliffs of Duncansby are not high by the standards of some of the cliffs within a few miles of them. A mere 210 feet is the highest point, yet there is something special in the clean-cut aspect which the Head of Duncansby presents to the sea, something calm about the horizontal striations of its strata and the sheer vertical of its thrust. The sense of calm is, however, entirely lost the moment one moves away from the Head, and sets one's eyes on the cliff scenery and seascapes to the immediate south. The *veruvium promontarium*, the 'clear-cut promontory' of the ancients, disappears in a tangle of wild formations which the sea has created out of the same sandstones, and here the predominant geological theme is that of sea stacks, which stand or lean like so many rotting teeth of some leviathan's jaw.

As you walk towards the southern headlands from which the stacks are most clearly seen, you rapidly learn that these are not the only geologically fascinating structures along these cliffs. Here, next to the headland beyond the lighthouse, is the natural bridge called the Glup, formed by a collapse where the sea has intruded into the cliff face. On the other side of the

The Duncansby Stacks, south of Dunnet head.

headland is an extensive geo, beyond which cliff abutment one has the first sight of the more famous stacks. From this point you can see the so-called Knee, a fine stack of regularly eroded limestone strata, some 70 feet above sea level, which is responsible for the distinctive tide race, locally called the Rispie.

Near the Knee is the most beautiful stack of the Duncansby giant teeth; separated from the cliff face by only a few yards, over 200 feet high, and with a most distinctive lean against the vertical, this is the Gibbs Craig, just round the corner from the beautiful shingles at the foot of Queenie Cliff. Further south of this shingle beach is a natural arch, called Thirle Door. From the green headland above this formation there is an impressive panorama of the main stacks of Duncansby – the Pedee Stack (perhaps a word from the French *petit*, 'small', as it is, in fact, when set against its brother beyond), protecting and dwarfing with its 218 feet the Tom Thumb Stack, behind which is the great Muckle Stack, rearing its mighty 297 feet beyond the cliffs.

A rather unlikely tale is told about Muckle Stack. The first man to climb it was a seventeenth-century tailor by the name of Ogston. It seems that during his climb he disturbed an eagle, which swooped down from its eyrie and attacked him. Curiously enough, he happened to be carrying his shears, and with these he stabbed at the eagle, drove it off and continued with his perilous climb.

Above: Muckle Stack in the foreground, Pedee Stack beyond, and the Tom Thumb stack down to the right.

Far left: The eroded cliffs and stacks of Duncansby, looking due north.

155

Dunnottar Fiddlehead

The conglomerates [of Dunnottar] form a rock of immense durability ... the cementing matter is so tough that faults or cracks which traverse the rocks are seen to pass not between the pebbles and their binding materials, but straight through the pebbles themselves.

W Douglas Simpson

Left: The castle of Dunnottar from the shingle of the south bay.

Right: A free-standing rock conglomerate, rising from the south bay shingle.

The restless fingers of the North Sea have slowly worked their destructive way around the rocks of Dunnottar to leave a distinctive peninsula wall, ending in a bulbous rock promontory, flanked on either side by shingle bays. This huge rock is held back to the mainland only by a high natural wall, a knife-edge causeway which would carry only a tight-rope walker to the castle beyond. The visual effect is astounding, and mainly because of such a majestic setting the historian J H Burton described this ruined castle in the last century as 'the most conspicuous stronghold along the east coast'.

The peninsula upon which this castle rests is over 160 feet high, poetically described as balancing four square upon the 'galled rock, O'erhand and butty his confounded base, Swilled with the wild and wasteful ocean'. More prosaically, the modern geologist will tell you that Dunnottar Castle has been built on top of a cliff of sandstone conglomerates which are in these parts of Scotland over 6,900 feet thick, and which point to deposits laid down hundreds of millions of years ago.

The knife-edge of rock which pulls the castle back to the mainland is almost perpendicular on both sides, and its wonder is contained in the beauty of its composition rather than in its shape, which has led to its being called the Fiddlehead. It consists of an incredible number of ancient pebbles and stones which are cemented together by natural means, the whole conglomerate forming, as the historian W D Simpson says, 'a rock of immense durability'. The photograph of a small section of this conglomerate indicates, more clearly than words may, the truth of what Simpson says about cracks passing through the pebbles. The sheer beauty of the coloured veins of these pebbles is breathtaking – certainly it is hard to believe that they are not made by artists of genius.

In common speech they are called 'pudding stones', a reference no doubt to the idea that

this mixture of rocks, pebbles and redstone cement is nothing more than a gigantic cake-mix. Here at Dunnottar this massive cookery is in fact a mere outcropping of vast areas of conglomerates, resting almost on the edge of that most famous of British geological formations, the Highland Boundary Fault, which breaks into the sea at Garron Point, only two miles north of nearby Stonehaven.

Due to extraordinary perturbations these conglomerate deposits have been thrown from their natural horizontal to a quite unnatural vertical. Thus, in leaning back to study the wall of the Fiddlehead, with its exquisite veinings, textures

and colours, we ourselves are in a sense thrown out of our vertical position and become like floating gods, looking down on ancient alluvial deposits.

In recent historical times a tunnel has been cut through a wall spur. With untold love and labour, a former caretaker of the castle worked in what Simpson, in his official guide, described as 'a laborious futility'. Some say that this man chipped away with his hammer and chisel because he wanted to carve within the rock a house for himself, but history does not record the reasons for this labour. There must be few places in the world more romantic for the

construction of a dwelling than in this spur which divided two lovely shingle beaches!

The beaches are themselves natural wonders, slowly inching their way to surround permanently the rocky promontory, and slowly collecting pebbles loosed from the grip of the conglomerate. To the north is Castle Haven, to the south, Old Hall Bay. The rich veining and multicoloured hues of the pebbles on this part of the Scottish coastline are almost beyond belief, and of course the salt waves' moisture brings out the colours in the highest refinement of sensitivity. The finest are to be had either from these shingles which fringe Dunnottar, or

from Lunan Bay or (best of all) from the scarcely visited shingle of Bervie Bay at Inverbervie, further south.

Our attention has been so drawn by the building of nature that we have ignored the human buildings on the rock; yet here is a castle with a history that parallels that of Scotland, even though the geological majesty of this area renders the acts of man pale and ephemeral.

An early Christian settlement was certainly here on this rock, for these people have left their symbols scratched upon stones, and records suggest that in the fifth century St Ninian had a church at Dunnottar. Then came many cruel

harryings of the north by waves of invaders, and in their turn the Vikings and the English (under Aethelstan) stood upon the rock to celebrate brief victories. The Scottish regalia were hidden here during the Civil Wars, when Cromwell's men were fooled by the courage of the minister's wife, who carried the crown beneath her skirts. Here there were also witch hunts – more savage in these parts than even those in England – and religious persecutions.

It is a chilling thought that nature wrenched herself in such perturbation, shifted the axis of whole strata, suffered the workings of seas both tropical and ice-bound, to build a rocky platform in support of such a parade of wrath, cupidity and rapine.

Above: A detail shows the colourful composition of the conglomerate upon which the castle is built.

159

Glencoe

I cannot attempt to describe the mountains [of Glencoe] . . . I can only say that I thought those on our right . . . were the grandest I had ever seen. It seldom happens that mountains in a very clear air look exceedingly high, but these, though we could see the whole of them to their summits, appeared to me more majestic in their own nakedness than our imaginations could have conceived them to be.

Dorothy Wordsworth

The western view of Glencoe from below the main road.

In her poetic description of the journey she and her famous brother made through Glencoe in 1803, Dorothy Wordsworth remarks on the difficulty they had in the valley. The rough road 'frequently crossed large streams of stones, left by the mountain-torrents, losing appearance of a road'. In modern times this wild Glencoe is tamed a little, for in spite of the efforts of conservationists, a good road runs the whole length, as though foolishly attempting to persuade the traveller to merely pass through the Glen and not to explore the wilderness on either side. You can still see the river with the same eyes as Dorothy, 'hidden between steep rocks . . . foaming over stones, or lodged in dark black dens', hedged in by mountains which Dorothy first praised, and then later scorned for being the 'images of terror' they had experienced in the Alps!

Glencoe itself is just over seven miles long, from Col to Loch Leven, and provides scenery as romantic as you could expect to find anywhere in the world. The valley proper opens to a fanfare of waterfalls, at the meeting of the three waters, pouring a series of savage falls into the river Coe as it rushes on to Loch Achtiochtan. These falls are generally admired by the tourists from the security of the road, but they are best seen by climbing up among them, and standing below the distinctive peaks of Buachaille Etive Mor, 'a huge pyramidal mountain' as Dorothy Wordsworth called it, the Great Shepherd of Etive, which marks the end of Glen Etive, the beginning of Glencoe. On the other side of the road from these waterfalls is the curiously named 'Study' – a rock platform from which the majority of tourists scan the panorama of the Glen. This Study is not merely a point from which to study the glen, as one might reasonably expect, but an awkward anglicization of the old Scots word for anvil, *stiddie*, which recalls its shape.

On the far side, the 'Three Sisters' stand sentinel to the south of Glencoe, carrying their

lovely Gaelic names Aonach Dubh, Gearr Aonach and Beinn Fhada, the scree at their toes edging continually onto the river Coe and Loch Achtriochtan. To the north of the Glen, facing on to these Sisters, is the craggy Notched Ridge, rearing its 3,000 feet for about six miles of the pass, sundered by deep gorges. To the west are green fields, still swathed in by the ring of mountains on all sides, but a welcome breath of air in all this immensity. In these fields, near Achnacon, the popular history of Glencoe begins, with a fire signal in February 1692, which led to the Glencoe Massacre.

Above Loch Triochtan towers the bleak Aonach Dubh, with a famous cave named after the legendary Gaelic hero, Ossian, who, if he lived at all, could not have inhabited this high cave, as anyone who has the stomach to climb to its steeply sloping floor will soon discover. Behind this massive mountain is a so-called 'Hidden Valley', the Coire Gabhail, a wrong translation seemingly encouraged by the tourist trade; the real name is more historical, however, if less romantic, for it evokes the actual business of the past clans in its meaning 'corrie of capture'. It was here, over a thousand feet above the Glen, that the MacDonalds would drive the cattle they owned by law, or (more

Left: The southern side of Glencoe's savage walls.

Above right: The spume at the meeting of the three waters, where the eastern entry into Glencoe begins.

Right: The range of mountains to the north of the western end of Glencoe.

often) by unwilling proxy, away from the prying eyes of others.

The distinctive form of Glencoe is essentially that of a huge cauldron. Geologists use precisely this word to describe the effect of a continuous circle of the magmatic volcanic action breaking through a vast ring fault, as though the earth within were a loose cork or plug. Such a break creates at first a vast walled dyke of lava, which finally hardens to a rock surface of mountains that circle the ancient plug; these later succumb to the slow actions of glaciers, wind and rain. In Glencoe, such petrified rock life, dating back to the oldest Dalradian period (over a thousand million years ago), combines with the geologically recent appin limestone and phylites. Yet, for all its complexity of form, we may still see around us the weathered structure of a ring of volcanic wall.

One might well understand why early conservationists fought to defend this valley, for the road which conquered them certainly detracts from its grandeur. And yet, if one looks at Glencoe with the knowing eyes of the long term which geology affords, one will see that the road will not be there for long, and indeed it takes very little imagination to blot out in the mind's eye this strip of road from the distant floor of the valley.

Loch Lomond

... like a flash of images from another world.
Dorothy Wordsworth

Loch Lomond, looking north from Luss.

'We had not climbed far before we were stopped by a sudden burst of prospect, so singular and beautiful that it was like a flash of images from another world ... What I had heard of Loch Lomond, or any other place in Great Britain, had given me no idea of anything like what we beheld: it was an outlandish scene.' Many tourists and travellers must have echoed these sentiments, set down by Dorothy Wordsworth in her journal during her visit to the Loch in 1803 in the company of her brother and Coleridge. The Loch is not only the largest of the inland waters of Britain, it is also the most beautiful and strange. As we wander along the banks or on its islands, we are left with the sensation that we might at any moment find ourselves stepping from this familiar world into another, richer one. Perhaps this is what Dorothy had in mind when she used the word 'outlandish' to describe her astonishment at the scene.

Loch Lomond is about 24 miles long, and at its widest point some five miles broad, narrowing down to less than a mile in places. The glaciers which gouged out the rocks to make the depression of Loch Lomond left a deep incision in the hard schist, inched around the harder deposits of grit, and merely scraped the softer sandstones. Loch Lomond still reflects this ancient bulldozing, for it is deep and ravined in the north, shallower and wider in the south, and has some thirty wooded islands throughout. The narrow, fjord-like gouge near Tarbet is 600 feet deep, while the Luss basin is a wide expanse less than 100 feet deep.

Its size is perhaps easy to describe, its form relatively easy to explain – but who may do justice to its beauty? There is a guidebook Loch Lomond, with startling blue skies which spread an azure sheen over the waters – a Loch described (even in the seventeenth century, before a taste for such things had really developed) as 'a small mediterranean surrounded with woods'. Then there is the sullen dark

Ben Lomond from across the Loch, through the distorting light of a rainbow.

Loch, with gathering storm clouds, which sweep down from the mountains and in a moment or two transform its sun-drenched beauty into a thing of dark shades, followed by rain-laden air which even in the darkest times may create a magic of rainbows over the waters. In summer there are multifoliate subtleties of waterlilies, and the delicate fantasy of the lagoons; in the winter the waters are alive with the din of geese and ducks, along with other curious vagrants. All the year round one can be surprised by a strange variety of bird life – even the occasional glimpse of the rare ospreys, which leisurely choose the larger fish from the teeming Loch.

If the view from below is varied and beautiful,

so are the panoramas from above. Although Ben Lomond does not tower directly over the Loch, its reticent peak is still distinctive on the northern side from Tarbet, and the magnificent views from its 3,192-foot summit take in the Firth of Clyde, the Arran Hills and the Antrim coast – even the Hebrides, and the distant peaks of Mull. The indefatigable Victorian climber Sir Hugh Monro, who made the ascent of all but two of the Scottish peaks, said that Ben Lomond gave the finest view of them all. It was, indeed, Sir Hugh who gave the name 'munro' to the natural formation which is seen to such advantage in the westward view of Loch Lomond – the munro being a hill of 3,000 or more feet, separated from another of like size by a depression of at least 500 feet.

The biggest island on the Loch is Inchmurrin, but Inchcailloch, the 'island of women', is the holy island. It was probably regarded as holy even before St Kentigerna opened her nunnery there in the eighth century, when the Celts were reinvigorating a decadent and world-weary Europe with Christianity. The church in her honour still raises its broken stones out of the soil, alongside the gravestones to the multitudinous dead of the MacGregors.

The beauty of this place is almost beyond belief, as are the statistics which lie behind it. So vast is this valley of water that it can be drained of a hundred million gallons a day by the Central Scotland Water Development Board, and yet still retain the same water level, which is adjusted by the mountain-fed streams and rivulets. One almost feels that there was a sense of purpose behind those vast ice flows of the past which carved this mountainous beauty. Were it not for the glacial deposits which they left behind the seas might have pushed into this long lake, making it a sea-fjord, or a tidal river with a structure and ecology very different from the surface of beauty we now enjoy. The Loch remains with its calm surface of blues and greens which is really a cosmetic to cover a slash gouged into the rocks millions of years ago.

Above: The Loch from the south-west, north of Luss.

Below: A point on the Loch favoured by William Wordsworth.

Mull

Of these Islands it must be confessed, that they have not many allurements, but to the mere lover of naked nature.

James Boswell

The famous tour which Boswell and Samuel Johnson made through the Hebrides makes infuriating reading for the modern nature-lover. Neither of them was apparently able to appreciate nature in the way we take for granted. It was as though they journeyed over these miraculous isles with blinkers on, with eyes only for the people and social conditions, quoting freely from Roman authors in a sort of academic slapstick, but blind to the beauty around them. It took the romantic revolution of the next century to open the eyes and minds of people to the beauty of wilderness, of 'nature in disarray'. In fact, the isle of Mull was, for Johnson, so pervaded with 'gloom and desolation' that he planned to relieve the austerity by planting trees over its entire surface.

Mull was once no island at all, but part of the Scottish mainland. Now you must take a ferry to reach the island – or, if possessed of the same desperate courage and hunger, attempt to wade at low tide, as did David Balfour, the hero of *Kidnapped*, or even swim, like the first crofters. But whichever route or method of travel you take, the crossing will surely be worthwhile.

How can one determine which of the many treasures on Mull should stand as representative of the island? There is a 50-foot fossil tree at Ardmeanach, which is said to be 50 million years old. There are many waterfalls, the majority of which are really steep rivulets streaming down the mountains, etching their way to the never-distant sea. Or one could choose one of the mountains, such as the highest peak of Ben More, or perhaps a loch, such as Loch an Keal, beloved of the seals – or even one of the varied ranges of cliffs, such as those at Carsaig, which are splendid basaltic rock formations.

The Ardmeanach fossil tree has sadly been largely removed. It has been stripped away, first by the slow motion of nature, and then, with greater rapidity, and with even greater thoroughness, by modern fossil collectors. Almost all that remains is the imprint of its form

Streams of water pour down the hillsides to the south of the Ross of Mull – a characteristic sight in Mull during heavy rain.

still preserved within the vertical lava bed.

Ben More, a lonely peak guarding Loch Scidain, stands high for such a small island, at 3,169 feet, and is indeed marvellous in its weathering. Yet, in comparison with other Scottish mountains, it cannot justly be termed a wonder. The cliffs of Gribun recall those of St John at Hoy, yet they do not have the same vertical dignity. The Carsaig cliffs have basaltic hexagonal columns almost as splendid as those at Staffa, or County Antrim, yet they are not so numerous nor are they so artistically formed.

But the real natural splendour of Mull is, to my mind, the rocks which crown the strands and beaches, as though huddled in silent protest at the raging of the Atlantic breakers. These at Fionnphort pictured here magically combine the eternal with the ephemeral, for they are wrapped in the warmth of a pink sunlight; so much hard earth matter transmuted into gold. These rocks would form a fitting backcloth for scenes in Shakespeare's *Tempest*: yet, save for the sound of the waves, Mull is a quiet place.

Mull boasts one further, although ephemeral, wonder and that is its sunset. The sunset over most of the Hebridean Islands often brings a *frisson*, perhaps because the sun sinks so starkly against a clear western sky, yet its setting over Mull is a very special thing. The golden body of

Left: Boulders on the beach a few yards beyond Fionnphort, given a transient beauty by the sunlight.

Below: Sunset over Mull, seen in the wake of the ferry.

the sun glides down behind the hills with strange rapidity, and with the same quite perceptible speed that can be seen in lonely deserts. First a fine haze of pink washes over the whole sky, so that for an hour or so before night the whole isle is diffused with an unearthly warm hue, then the pyrotechnics begin, and the skies are flooded with blood crimsons, intense yellows and the clash of contrasting purples before all merges into a sudden darkness. The glory lasts for only a few minutes, but will live forever in the heart of anyone who is there to witness it. Is it possible that Dr Johnson could have traversed the whole of Mull, during his days upon the island, without being stirred by such a sight?

Above: The fantastic rock protuberances on the shores near Fionnphort.

171

The Old Man of Hoy

The island of Hoy is a rampart for the others, concealing them from view, and like a sentinel before its cliffs, isolated by the waves that break to whiteness on its base, is the tall and brooding stack, ruddy of hue, called The Old Man of Hoy.
Eric Linklater

The Old Man of Hoy from the southern cliffs. It is possible to climb halfway down these cliffs by way of a collapsed sea-cave, but the route is dangerous.

The ancients, on the advice of the philosopher Epictetus, held it the duty of all men to visit the Statue of Zeus at Olympia, one of the Seven Wonders of the Ancient World. It was regarded by them as a tragedy if a man should die without having seen this miracle of art. I would make the same claim for the Old Man of Hoy, and insist that every Briton should see it at least once in a lifetime, for it is surely the most wonderful sight in our isles.

A journey to see the Old Man of Hoy is something akin to a pilgrimage which starts out with a sense of disappointment, yet which leaves one in the end virtually gasping in amazement. The first view of the Old Man is usually from the boat, seen to the east on the way to the Orkneys. From such a distance, it is a small column at first, edging slightly over the cliff face to its right, which one knows to be over five hundred feet high, but which from the boat looks diminutive. The waves 'break to whiteness on its base', and flurry a white powder of spray along the cliffs of St John to the north which completely dominate the stack with their breathtaking 1,100 feet. It is a beautiful sight, especially when the cliffs are swirled in mist and reduced to transparent blues and purples by sea fog, but it is not quite as impressive as one might at first have hoped. The scale is wrong. At this point you can scarcely be blamed for turning away from the long journey ahead: it will be easier to visit the other sea-stack of the Orkneys at Yesnaby, and there will be no sense of disappointment there.

But if the first sight is sufficient encouragement to persuade you to continue to the foot of the Old Man, then you will find yourself rewarded in a most unexpected way. Most of the distance you will be carried, first by boat to Mainland from the Scottish coast at Scrabster, and next by a smaller boat to the island of Hoy. Then there is a long walk, or a car ride for the lucky, to the scarcely visited hamlet of Rackwick, followed by a two-mile uphill slog to the

The Old Man seen from the north – one of the most spectacular views. The climb down from this cliff is relatively easy, but the view upwards from the shore is disappointing, as little of the Old Man can be seen.

174

cliffs which gave birth to the Old Man. And there, as you approach the seaward edge of the cliffs, the stack salutes you as before: it appears as an unimpressive high mound standing above the cliff face, a few feet higher than the turf. Thus it is seen at a distance of a few hundred yards.

Gradually you make your way across the boggy ground towards the cliff edge, and the Old Man begins to raise himself. The experience is quite uncanny, for as you move towards the stack you look down into an ever deepening precipice between cliff and stack, and with every further step you feel that you must have finally seen the bottom of this extraordinary column of stratified rock. But no, the plunge continues, until you feel literally quite giddy, and need something to grasp on to – but there is nothing to hold! You are standing on the very edge of the cliff, and still you must peer over to see the rocky pedestal upon which this stack is raised.

To do justice to this 450-foot-high stack, photography must ignore the precipice, and show the column's relationship to the cliff from which it has broken loose. To take such a picture requires that one climbs down the cliff face to the left or to the right of the stack – both dangerous enterprises and best not attempted at all. The better view is the one from the south, and fortunately the climb on this side is made a little easier by the fact that in ages past a cave roof must have collapsed, leaving a natural depression which may be negotiated from the top of the cliffs with only a short climb.

The Old Man stands as though in proclamation of Hoy's name, which means 'high' in old Norse. Yet the ancient voyagers could not have seen the Old Man himself as we do now, for geologically speaking he is merely a child, as he was left free-standing by a cliff fall only about three centuries ago.

The flat dark pedestal of older basalt which supports the lank body of the stack is one of the distinguishing features of the geology of the Hoy cliffs, and may be traced in the higher cliffs of St John, further west. The Old Man is the highest sea-stack in Great Britain, yet even he is dwarfed by the vertical sublimity of St John's Head, where the red and yellow sandstones, topped by the green grasses, rise over twice his height.

The modern fame of the Old Man is partly derived from the media, for BBC television filmed a successful climb of the stack in 1967, and the results are seen on both the stack and on the mainland of Hoy. This televised climb of 1967, led by Hamish McInnes, was not, how-

Above: From the sea the Old Man is dwarfed by the mist-shrouded cliffs of St John's, which are well over twice its height.

ever, the first climb of the Old Man, as is generally believed, for Chris Bonnington led a team to the top in the previous year – a feat which no doubt encouraged the media to its own enterprise. Chris Bonnington left a cairn there to commemorate his climb, and this (some five or six feet high) can be seen in all modern photographs, and gives some concept of the real scale of this stratified monster.

The small island of Hoy is a delight of flowers, and indeed, because of the alpine flowers which mingle with popular British strains, it is sometimes referred to as the 'botanic treasury' of the Orkneys. A most curious relic of the past – made famous by an indifferent novel by Sir Walter Scott – is the Dwarfie Stone, which has nothing to do with dwarfs but with an ancient race of men. This stone, which can be seen to the left of the single road to Rackwick, is a wonder in itself – a long block of hard sandstone, about 28 feet long, 13 feet deep and 7 high. It is famed because it is one of the only two known rock-cut tombs in the British Isles. The cut chambers within are small, yet exquisitely formed, and are said to date back to the fourth millennium BC. The setting is superb, placed as it is against the volcanic remains which make up this island of Hoy, a stone pigmy in the land of the Old Man giant.

Above: The megalithic Dwarfie Stone on Hoy.

Left: The Old Man from the southern cliffs.

Right: The astounding cliffs to the north of the Old Man gradually build up to a height of over a thousand feet.

Left: The entrance
to Fingal's Cave
resembles the portal
of a mediaeval
church.

Below: The
pavement of basalt
columns between
Am Buachaille and
Fingal's Cave.

Staffa

Fingal's Cave, Cormorant's Cave, Clamshell Cave, Bird Island, Am Buachaille, the 'Herdsman' ... even the names of the geological formations on the remarkable island of Staffa, set majestically to the west of Mull in defiance of the wild Atlantic waves, breathe a romance, a music to the soul. Though entirely the product of the movements of the earth, there is something unearthly in the strange caves and pavements of this enchanted isle, as though the gods had participated in its building.

The fishermen who first named the caves, rocks and promontories in the northern parts of Great Britain were convinced that the vast formations of the Giant's Causeway in Ireland and of the causeways, cliffs and caves of the island of Staffa were built by giants. They even identified the leader of this fanciful race, and called him Fin ma Cool, from which we have the modern name, Fingal. It is not surprising that such natural wonders should have been seen as works of architecture, and that one finds again and again opinions that the entire wondrous island of Staffa should have been built by giants, gods or even men. Everywhere on the island there are rock formations and caves which point to human artifice, rather than to the accidents of natural formations, and anyone who has visited the island and studied such formations must echo the words of the first official description which reckons it as 'one of the greatest natural curiosities in the world'.

The most famous spot on the island reminds one more of a mediaeval church facade, with pier clusters and triangular arch, than of a cave; this is, of course, Fingal's Cave, romanticized in 1832 by Mendelssohn in his overture. The geologists tell us that the architectonic precision of the basalt columns which frame the entrance to the cave (and of the so-called 'pavements' which connect Fingal's Cave to Clamshell Cave along the shore) was due to the fairly slow cooling of the basaltic lava flows in the Hebrides. The cooling took place under tremendous

pressure and, following a geological law which states that relief to a universal strain may be had only through triadic shearing, the extrusions formed hexagonal cross sections.

These sections are themselves more clearly seen on the pavements which lead around the island to Fingal's Cave, and the verticals of the basalt are most perfectly preserved around the entrance to the cave itself. The cave is 227 feet deep, 65 feet high (from mean tide level to apex of the arch), and 42 feet wide at the entrance. Such statistics are dry, for the feature of the cave is not its size, but the double interplay of the natural architecture and the sound of the waves

which so bewitch the ears. In his fascinating book on Staffa, Donald MacCulloch records that the pronunciation of the Gaelic for Fingal's Cave, Ua Bhin (oo-a-feen), is very little different in sound from the word meaning 'musical cave', and this might well have been the origin of even the Fingal legend.

The peculiar musical notes of the cave are generally explained as being a combination of the boom of waves and the pressure of sea water against an underwater air-hole – the impact and release of pressures gauged at several tons per square inch of surface has the effect of treating the huge air-hole as a sort of massive trumpet. This music and roar may under extreme conditions be of a terrifying proportion – it is said by locals that in time of storm the noises of Staffa may be heard as far away as the island of Geometra, four miles distant. An official report on the island (dated 1887) records that 'a shepherd and his family were persuaded to go on to the island, but they soon beseeched to be removed, because the hollow roar made by the sea through the caverns during times of storm sounded so dismally that they became terrified'.

It is extraordinary that such a wonder of the world should have remained unsung for so

Below: The basalt pavements and columns alongside the islet of Am Buachaille.

long. As an island it was of course known to early seafarers: indeed it was from the early visitors to the island that we derive its modern name, for the Norsemen called it *Staphi-ey*, 'the island of pillars'. It appears to have been inhabited for short periods (remains of rude buildings may still be seen), but no one has lived on the island for any length of time for well over a century. It was brought to the attention of the public by Sir Joseph Banks, who chanced upon it almost by accident whilst making a voyage to Iceland in 1772. His announcement of its remarkable formations immediately took a grip on the nascent Romanticism in Britain, with the result that it fired the imagination of many writers, poets and artists, including Turner, Sir Walter Scott, Keats, Wordsworth, Tennyson, James Hogg, and even Jules Verne. Dr Johnson and his faithful Boswell sought to visit the island, on their Hebridean journey, but the sea was too rough.

The sea was also rough two centuries later when I took the photograph of Staffa (opposite), almost silhouetted against the dark stub of Bird Island. On that trip it was impossible to land, the waves being far too heavy, and I was forced to continue the internal struggle I was having with seasickness as well as the external struggle with salt spray, which was ruining my camera lenses. Even on a peaceful, sunny day Bird Island is covered with a gentle white snow. In one of those rare moments when you can edge a boat near enough, the snow reveals itself as an organic, undulating mass of sea-birds, who whirl upwards in an angry foam of indignation and surprise at human invasion. By a curious accident of navigation, my first trip to Staffa brought me alongside Bird Island, and ever since that dramatic view of black rocks and white snows, I have harboured a secret longing to land there. Always, however, the lure of the green and magical Staffa has proved stronger.

The modern visitor will, of course, admire Fingal's Cave, and the surrounding organ pipes of basaltic columns which secure it to the sea, but there are, in fact, many natural beauties in this place, all of them in one way or another the artistic work of the cooling basalt.

Clamshell Cave is remarkable for the contrast of its extraordinary arch of basalt columns against the hexagonal stubs and columns around it. On one side of the beautifully proportioned curvature of the basalt columns which give the distinctive form of the raised 'clamshell' (suggesting the idea of an upturned hull of a huge boat) are the hexagonal columns of the 'organ pipes' which give Staffa its distinc-

tive form from the sea, while on the other side is a honeycomb structure of basalt stubs which gradually sweep upwards to the very top of the grasses on the top of the strange cliff. The cave itself is not easily accessible, but projects inwards some 130 feet, and is about 30 feet high at the mouth. James Hogg described the Clamshell in his lay of 1813, *The Abbot MacKinnon*:

Where furnaced pillars in order stand,
All formed of the liquid burning levin,
All bent like the bow that spans the Heaven.

To one side of the basalt pavement and the vertical columns of the so-called 'organ pipes', a few yards out to sea, is the thirty-foot-high Am Buachaille, an islet of basaltic columns and stubs. According to the more imaginative, this islet marks the place where the remnant columns were cast aside during the excavations of Fingal's Cave by the giants who built Staffa. If this is such a refuse tip, then the ancient giants disposed of their rubbish with great love and precision, for the islet is a work of art in itself, giving the impression of a disturbed honeycomb.

Almost opposite the Am Buachaille, set in the vertical columns which frame the cliffs, is a rough cavity which forms a sort of chair out of a series of hexagonal stubs. This appears to have been named in order to satisfy such tourists who were not already overwhelmed by Staffa itself: an entirely modern legend tells us that anyone sitting on this so-called 'Wishing Chair of Fingal' will have their wishes granted, but this is tourist-baiting, for the cavity has had different names in the past.

It is, of course, quite fascinating to walk along this pavement, and to brush against the amazing column walls – but the fact remains that the range of columns is best seen from the sea itself. From a boat it is possible to observe more clearly the inclination of the columns (at about seven degrees to the vertical) as well as the distinctive slope of the entire island (on a south-west to north-west line), which is no doubt due to the gradual sloping of the entire sea-bed.

An anonymous poem on Staffa, published in the first decade of the last century, saw this lovely island as the retreat of the Goddess of Nature, who is tired of the pride of human art. The poet describes it as 'Staffa's Isle, where Nature scoffs at Art!':

'Tis Nature's palace! scorning to abide
In temples less in reverence rear'd than pride;
The surges roar more grateful to the ear,
And tempest-hymn, than voice of hollow prayer;
She fled, disdainful of a Doric fane,
And built her minster on th'Atlantic main.

Yesnaby Castle

On the west coast of Mainland from Black Craig northwards there is a seemingly endless succession of headlands, bays and narrow trench-like inlets called geos, together with caves, gloups or blow-holes, arches and sea-stacks in every stage of development and destruction.

Patrick Bailey

It is little surprise that the jacket of the book *Orkney* from which this quotation was culled should display a colour picture of the wild coastline so described. Even less surprising, the picture is of that coastline's most wonderful sea-stack, called the Castle of Yesnaby.

The geology of the Orkneys is fascinating, something like a series of dramatic cinematographic 'stills' from an epic of cosmic proportions. You can even participate in this epic. If you stand on the hill of Brinkles Brae, on the west coast of Mainland, you will see before you two famous natural wonders – the sullen expanse of Scapa Flow and the volcanic hills of Hoy. Yet it is possible that you may be standing astride a third wonder. On this hill you find the oldest rock formations of the Orkneys, pre-Cambrian granite-schists; to the west are the fine reds of the sandstones. At certain points it is possible to stand across both of these, for the two striations are dramatically contiguous. If you do so, then you are bridging many millions of years and titanic foldings of the earth.

These 'stills' from the ancient drama are exhibited against a general tilting of the land against the horizontal sea – it is an effect observed more clearly in the sliding of the island of Staffa. Such dramatic scenery could only have been made by cataclysms which the mind can scarcely conceive. The forming of such land-tilts, sea-caves, stacks, blow-holes, natural arches, stumps, and faults which abound in this place are the result of vast upheavals, all of which can be seen as though frozen on this island.

Yesnaby Castle is the most impressive of all the natural formations on Mainland, located a few miles north of Stromness, just off a line of cliffs which offer walks as fine as any you will find in Britain. The natural arches and the blow-hole, the pounding of the waves as they sculpt the sandstones, are special in this place, but when the mists come (as they do frequently), then a true magic indeed is worked.

Yesnaby Castle from the south-east – its most distinctive silhouette.

weight, and that the whole seaward face might cave in – as, indeed, one day it surely will. This silhouette from the side is highly distinctive, and the one most represented in guidebooks. It is probably this outline which has helped make Yesnaby Castle so famous. There are several fine sea-stacks around these wild coasts, one of which competes in size at least with Yesnaby – the North Gaulton Castle, two miles further south along this coast, which stands 170 feet above the waves – yet it is not as striking as the Yesnaby stack.

The sunset also brings a touch of magic, and the westward view at these times weaves a romance of its own: the finest view of the castle is against a delicate sunset, when the golden or red disc gently touches the top of the stack, crowning it with a special glory.

The glory of the Orkney coastline is reflected inland, albeit in a less natural light, by a series of standing-stones. One of the most impressive of these stone circles is the Ring of Brogar, a few miles east of the Yesnaby stack. It has a diameter of 115 yards, and there are still 27 stones standing, although it was originally composed of 60 stones. Further inland is a smaller circle, which has twelve uprights. It now has only four, although they are among the highest in the island, one being over seventeen feet tall.

Above: Yesnaby Castle at sunset, the most romantic time in this myth-strewn part of the Orkneys.

Left: Standing-stones of Stenness on Mainland Orkney, a few miles east of the Yesnaby Castle.

Yesnaby Castle is best seen in a shrouding mist. Approached from the north, it is first visible as a thin flat-ended spire, some 180 feet above the waves, more like a church than any castle, and it is only when you have rounded the southern headland that its more familiar side can be observed. Seen from the south it demonstrates its name, for it is indeed like a fairy castle, with horizontal brick-like stratification of rocks and with a curious natural arch at the bottom which suggests in the mists the idea of a doorway, leading into the adventurous sea beyond. There is something precarious about the balance of this sea-eroded Yesnaby Castle, for one feels that the narrow column of the arch to the seaward side is carrying far too much

Right: An uncharacteristic view of the Yesnaby stack from the cliffs to the east.

WALES

PICTURE: SEA ARCH, ST GOVAN'S HEAD – SEE PAGE 207

Introduction

At the height of the greatest extension of the ice, there was not a single foot of Welsh soil that did not lie under this cold winding-sheet.
Wynford Vaughan-Thomas

Right, above: The panoramic view from the top of Cader Idris over the surrounding hills – one of the most lovely scenes in Wales.

Far right: A distinctive pinnacled arch in the amphitheatre of rocks which enclose St Govan's Chapel, Dyfed.

Right, below: Looking west towards the Cader and from precisely the same spot as the photo above. The pictures were taken within a few moments of each other – an indication of how rapidly the mists can descend.

All but Welshmen enter a foreign land when they step over the border into Wales. While there is no rugged line of mountains to mark the separation between England and this country, the very language, which is more song than speech, sets the people apart. The language permeates the air, and the very atmosphere is one of remoteness. It is as though the ice which carved out the rich lands of Wales remains there still in spirit, and for all the surface beauty of natural forms, there is an underlying chill. It is a land at times vibrant with a chilling intensity, at other times shrouded in mystery, yet always it is compelling in its wild beauty.

How can one, then, select without injustice only a few natural wonders in such a land? One could with little difficulty fill all these pages with the wonders of Snowdonia alone, yet this would be rank unfairness to the other great chains and peaks – to the hump backs of the Black Mountains and to a hundred other peaks, and to the many wonderful outcroppings which thrust out of this intense land.

Such a choice would also ignore the magnificent marine sculpture found in the Pembrokeshire coastlines, eroded in their defiance of the waves which surge through the Bristol Channel. Worst of all, such a limitation would leave out the waterfalls and this is a land of waterfalls, for just as the coastlines of Wales are constantly attacked by the ocean, so the countryside in the interior succumbs to the pressure of water from the skies, accelerated by the multitudes of peaks, and carried to the sea. Here, nature has again displayed her artistic talents in thousands of waterfalls – more falls than peaks – all bewitchingly different in shape, volume and depth.

To present the Snowdonia massif as the single wonder would be to show only the outer face of Wales, and to ignore the inner glories of the caves, which honeycomb vast areas, and the gorges, such as the Llanberis, for which the place is famous.

Left: One of the
many upright rocks
among the
outcropping at
Treffgarne, north of
Haverford.

Below: One of the
curious rock
formations at the
Treffgarne
outcroppings.

Thus, to solve this problem and to indicate the variety of natural wonders, I have chosen only one massif, Snowdonia – the richest park in the whole of Britain – one gorge, the breathtaking crevice and basins spanned by Devil's Bridge, and two related caves at Craig-y-nos, one containing the largest chamber of all showcaves in Britain, the other the most beautiful of systems. I have reduced the teeming riches of the miles of Pembrokeshire coastline to two small areas only, St Govan's Head, and the nearby Elegug Stacks, including a glance at the diverse natural formations within easy walking distance. Both these are symbols of Wales, for at St Govan's there is a chapel and at Elegug there is a bridge named after the country; both are now surrounded by a tank-training ground on one side and by the furious Atlantic rollers on the other. Yet the magic of these few miles of coastline is such that it still explains the ancient Welsh description of Pembrokeshire as *Gwlas yr Hud*, 'The land of enchantment'.

From among the hundreds of peaks that could have been selected, there arose the incomparable Cader Idris, whose intensity is easy to feel yet hard to fathom, and has given rise to many myths and mythologies.

The very number of Welsh waterfalls has justified a wider selection of this particular type

*Left: The west side
of the Snowdon
massif.*

*Below: One of the
main falls of the
Rheidol at Devil's
Bridge.*

of wonder, and three have insinuated themselves, almost without the asking. Yet they are each very different in form, force and spirit – the wide rapids of Swallow Falls, near Betws-y-Coed, the high narrow Pistyll Rhaeadr, with the unique interruption of a natural bridge, and the spectacular six cataracts at Devil's Bridge.

The chief delight of nature is that for once familiarity does not breed contempt, and one particular place may beckon one for personal reasons above all others. Because of this, my special love for the brooding dark ravine of swirling waters and for the lush woodlands of Devil's Bridge has taken me back to Wales in body and in memory time and time again.

'The foremost scenic attraction in mid-Wales' is how a recent official tourist guide has described the Bridge, and I must agree. Devil's Bridge reminded Wordsworth of the very beginning of the world, when all was young, and led him inevitably to think of his own ageing body; the place was so charged with intensity for George Borrow that he only dared contemplate it for three minutes, and advised the traveller to limit his time likewise. For myself, the natural beauty spread around these three bridges also romantically reminds me of youth and of all that is alive – yet I feel that I could contemplate it for centuries without a moment of boredom.

193

Cader Idris

The appeal of Cader Idris – the so-called 'Arthur's Chair' – rests on its wild romance, rather than upon its height or the majesty of its peaks. Its 2,970-foot summit scrapes the skies with the solemn ridge of Craig Lwyd, a 'sharp crag' which rises above the silent depths of the dark lake Llyn Cau, in a perfect union of rocks and water.

It is not surprising that the early Romantic artists should have been gripped by wild intensities of mood when seeing the Cader. Making a journey around Wales in 1856, Tennyson wrote in his diary that he 'never saw anything more awful than the great veil of rain drawn straight over Cader Idris, pale light at its lower edge. It looked as if death were behind it, and made me shudder when I thought he was there.' This is a very different vision of the Cader to one with serene golden light as portrayed by Richard Wilson in a picture in the National Gallery, London, which has done more than any other single thing to create an image of this lake and peak. Such contrasts in vision should remind us that all mountains have many faces. But whether bathed in a Wilsonian golden light or swathed in mists and fogs, in both extremes there is something quite uncanny and powerful about the place.

The three main peaks, visible from the approach road from Dolgellau, are the Tyrau Mawr, the saddle Cyfrwy, and Pen y Gadair. It is probably an imaginative view of these that has given rise to the idea of a gigantic chair, though if one has to think of a chair at all, then the lake could be its seat with the encircling peaks as its back and armrests. A mighty giant would be comfortable in such a soft chair, were it not for the fact that linguistic experts long ago threw out the giant, as well as the popular notion that Cader means 'chair', and it now seems that the word Idris never meant 'Arthur'. Equally dubious is the suggestion that Idris was a kinsman of the Celtic chief Cunedda, killed in a historic battle in the seventh century, and the

Cader Idris, swathed in mists, well evokes the sombre mythology of the Welsh mountains.

Above: The silent and threatening lake of Llyn Cau at the foot of the Cader peak.

Far right: Cader Idris from the north-west.

name remains as much a mystery as the mountain itself.

The warm vision of Richard Wilson's painting may never leave our minds when looking at the water-filled chasm of Llyn Cau (understandably said to be bottomless), contrasting its smooth circle against the sheer rough ridge of the peak which towers some twelve hundred feet above. The painting is sun-filled, and it is indeed true that in the late afternoon the summit does cup the sun in a most cunning way, reflecting its pure gold on the peaks. Yet the spirit of Wales is somehow not in the golden sun but in the blue green mists, and here at the Cader one can watch in astonishment the rapidity with which such mists swathe their blue gloom over a sunlit

scene, the greys swirling down like a formless dragon. Wales is a land of such dissolving mists, as though the land itself was formed before the sun was born, and never entirely solidified or took on any concrete shape like the rest of the world.

This swirling spectacle and its subtle kaleidoscopic changes can be watched from one of the natural tiers of rock above the marshland in front of the lake. Such a sight will explain the legend that anyone who spends the night on the Cader will, by the following morning, be either a bard or a lunatic. These are ideas redolent of Shakespeare, but for sure the very wildness of the scene could well draw from out of the deep recesses of the human sensibility the

encourage such fantasizing, as the contrast with the still deep waters of the lake, natural symbol of the subconscious powers lurking in every man. The lake of Llyn Cau has, of course, been peopled with monsters and, faced with such brooding intensity it is perhaps not difficult to imagine the hidden creature which devours whole those who attempt to swim across the dark surface.

Almost every one of the many lakes and pools of Wales has been bequeathed a monster, from the sinister Afranc, which once lived in the Lyn yr Afranc on the Conwy (but which was finally trapped and thrown into the Green Lake of Glaslyn), to less imaginative tales told by travellers who have claimed to witness the devastations of such creatures, as here in Llyn Cau. However, faced with the mist-laden splendour of the drear face of Cader Idris, one feels that here, as with all places that invoke powerful imaginings, one should not come too close, for in such a lake there must be a creature, even if it lives only within the human imagination, and surely the watery depths *do* penetrate far down into the earth. For here is the stuff not only of unbridled romanticism, but of Welsh demonology itself.

creative powers which pour forth in song or rhyme. The very word 'lunatic' from the Latin for moon, *luna*, makes curious sense in this setting, for it is so lunar in its rocks and boulders that it is with astonishment that one sees the flat and forbiddingly quiet waters of the Llyn, as the moon itself is waterless. Yet, this delightful and appropriate conceit, which makes of the unwary night traveller a bard or a lunatic, is a literary device. It can be traced only to the last century, and the dubious pen of Mrs Hemans, who created a legend as enduring to the romantic mind as the painting by Wilson, and as difficult for the traveller to this peak to throw off.

However, it is not so much the peaks which

Dan-yr-Ogof
and Cathedral Cave

At the far end of the lake ... there are a number of further formations. That to the left at floor level closely resembles the tracery of a mediaeval church screen although some visitors see in it a repeat of the organ pipe pattern whilst to others it represents classical columns or a wedding cake.

A C Coase

When the early chroniclers of Wales drew up their lists of the 'seven wonders' of their country – intending no doubt to compete with the wonders of the ancient world – they did not know of the mysteries and beauties of the two cave systems of Craig-y-nos, south of the Brecon Beacons. Had they known these, then they would doubtlessly have included them in their list, for they are wonders indeed. Discovered and investigated in the first half of this century, these caves are now partly open to the public, grouped under the names of Dan-yr-Ogof and the Cathedral Cave. They should be included in any modern list of natural wonders, for they are regarded as being among the finest show-caves in Great Britain.

Dan-yr-Ogof means 'below the cave', and, as the name indicates, the system is actually below another large cave, called Ogof-yr-Esgyrn. As archaeological researches have shown, this one had been known for centuries. To the side of the cave entrance, the River Llynfell emerges after a four-mile underground journey, part of it through the caves beyond – a journey which takes the water anything from two to three days, depending upon the weather conditions.

Show-caves are generally designed with tourism in mind, which explains why their natural formations are given names as though nature were herself somehow interested in realism. The cave of Dan-yr-Ogof is no exception to this unfortunate rule, and it grates on the ears to be told that certain stalactites are 'parrots', others 'carrots', or that a 'belfry' of slowly moulded flowstone is actually a 'frozen waterfall', when this is neither true nor particularly imaginative. As Howell and Beazley somewhat contemptuously put it in *A Companion Guide to North Wales*, 'A Group of Nuns stand close to a Broody Hen'! But such flights of fancy aside, the cave is impressive in its wide display of varied stalactites, stalagmites, columns, flow-stones, bridges, caverns, and underground water systems, including lakes and falls.

'Straws', or thin stalactites, may be seen in fair abundance throughout the system, but few of them are very long: the finest selection is found in those parts of the cave accessible only to seasoned pot-holers.

Perhaps the most outstanding formation is the 'Flitch of Bacon', a hanging curtain of calcite which is fortunately near enough to the ground level of the cave to permit easy inspection. This calcite is translucent, and has been back-lit in order to reveal its natural striations of colour – mainly reds against yellows, with a delicate tracery of water still imperceptibly depositing calcium carbonate on the bottom rim of the Flitch. Such curtains are, like the stalactites, formed by slow calcite deposit, but are a result

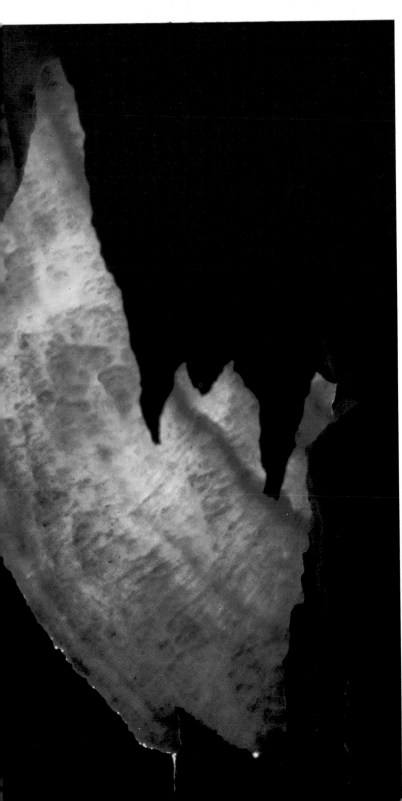

of a slow flow of water along a sharp edge, rather than a vertical dripping. This action leaves a linear, semi-horizontal deposit of calcite, which then in turn becomes a recipient for a similar slow flow of water; imperceptibly a knife-edge, inclined to the vertical, is thrust downwards, eventually to form a curtain-like sheet. Stratification colours appear in such curtains due to the presence within the calcite deposit of trace minerals (and sometimes of organic elements) carried from the rocks by the river and waterfalls. For example, the lovely reds, which predominate in the Flitch of Bacon, are derived mainly from traces of iron salts.

Another interesting formation within the show-cave is the so-called Alabaster Pillar, which is actually a column of calcite, made from the gradual joining of a stalactite with its related lower stalagmite. The whole stands – or drops – some six feet high, yet this is magnified to almost twice the size by its perfect reflection in the shallow sheet of water which lies around its base.

Towards the end of the show-cave system is the Cauldron Chamber, which contains a small waterfall at floor level, and an extraordinary blanket of calcite high in the cave roof. Once again, special lighting has been installed to reveal the translucent beauty of this draped sheet, which is about eighteen feet in length and is said to be the biggest in any show-cave in Britain. Its colour striations and loose-looking folds give the impression of a draped Algerian blanket, petrified in the air.

Almost all the natural formations within Dan-yr-Ogof – especially the stalactites and the curtains – have been protected in recent years by wire mesh screens. This has unfortunately detracted from the enjoyment of the many formations, but vandalism and theft have become such a problem that, as one guide said to me laconically, 'no screens, no stalactites'. However, it has not been found necessary to protect the flowstones with wire mesh, so their peculiar beauty may be seen quite easily. Flow-stones are 'frozen waterfalls': they are actually created by sheet flows of calcite, first over rocks, and then over the strata of calcite sheets. A curious archaeological find in the Ogof-yr-Esgyrn cave, above the Dan-yr-Ogof system, has enabled geologists to date with fair accuracy the time involved in such formations of local flowstones. A shard of Roman pottery was discovered buried some three inches below the flow of a calcite petrification, suggesting a building process of three inches in about 1,800 years – or something in the order of the thickness of a human thumbnail every decade!

The Cathedral Cave, which is to the right, and slightly higher than the Dan-yr-Ogof system, was thought until comparatively recently to be a fairly uninteresting cave; it was believed to be no more than four feet in height, and to penetrate some 150 feet into the hillside as far as a complete choke of boulders. Since the cave was often completely filled with water, it attracted little attention until cavers observed draughts issuing from the far end – a fair indication that exploration might be rewarded by the discovery of an unknown system. By the end of 1953 the South Wales Caving Club had taken exploration and controlled explosive blasting far enough to break into the huge body of what is now called the Cathedral Cave – the largest illuminated chamber in any British show-cave.

It is probably the vast size of this space which has evoked the popular name, but there are also within it numerous calcite formations to which imagination might accord ecclesiastical significance. Among these are the so-called 'Organ Pipes', a massive wall display of limestone stalactites and pillars with vertically indented fluting, which are somewhat reminiscent of the basaltic columns of Staffa. A smaller area of stalactites and stalagmites nearby are said by

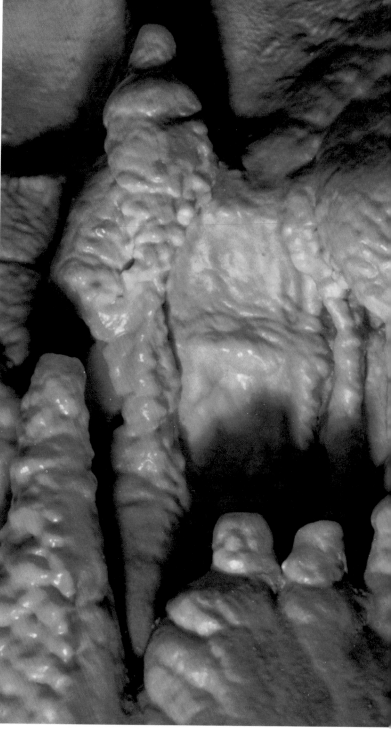

Above: Stalagmites against a backdrop of calcite flow-stones in the Cathedral Cave system.

Left: Stalagmites and flow-stones combined on the wall of the Cathedral Cave.

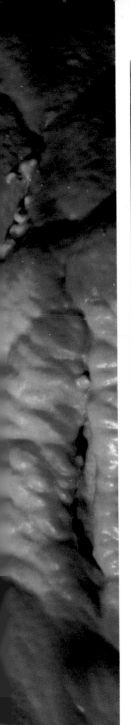

Left: A curtain of calcite high in the ceiling of the Cauldron Chamber in the Dan-yr-Ogof system.

the guides to resemble a 'choir', resplendent with 'choir-boys', yet, beautiful as these natural wonders are, a strong imagination is required to read such significance into them.

Within the huge chamber of the Cathedral Cave are delightful flowstones, multi-coloured stalactites, columns, natural waterfalls (as well as pump-fed artificial waterfalls) and lakes. A narrow gorge-like twist within the cave leads into the 'Dome of St Paul's', as high as the cupola of the famous cathedral in London (excluding the golden gallery and lantern), though not of so great a volume.

Displayed within the show-cave is a boulder of coral limestone which was dredged from the river Llynfell within the Dan-yr-Ogof system –

evidence of the tropical seas which covered this area about 300 million years ago. Alongside this specimen is a fossil sample of the Calamites, a tree which grew in the swamps following the subsidence of those warm seas, some millions of years later.

As with the Dan-yr-Ogof system, the Cathedral Cave continues well beyond the limits of the present lighted system open to the public, and indeed the network of passages beyond are still being explored, with reasonable anticipation of comparable wonders being revealed in the future. A water-filled sump, called the Flood Rising, was explored by a caver in 1954, although further exploration here eventually led to a blockage of boulders.

Devil's Bridge

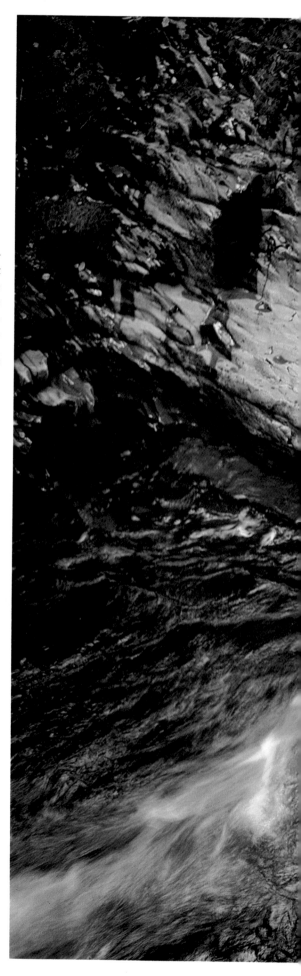

And if pleasant recollections do not haunt you through life of the noble falls and the beautiful wooded dingles to the west of the bridge of the Evil One ... I say boldly that you must be a very unpoetic person indeed.

George Borrow

The water-worn Devil's Punchbowl at the base of the volcanic chasm and below the three bridges of Devil's Bridge.

The Devil's Bridge, a few miles east of Aberystwyth, spans the River Mynach, where it meets the Rheidol, and keeps apart two of the great sights of Wales. Immediately below the bridges is a dark volcanic cleft which sinks into the Devil's Punch Bowl; a few yards beyond, to the west, is a beautiful 500-foot gorge in which the falls of the Rheidol stream in a series of cataracts some 300 feet into a wooded basin below.

Devil's Bridge, sentinel to these two wonders, is inaptly named. It was begun by Benedictine monks, and the lowest of the three arches is still memorial to this monkish labour; the earliest record of its historic existence is from the pen of Giraldus of Wales, when he passed over the bridge in 1180. The monks who built it are themselves woven into the texture of Welsh history, for they were said to be in charge of the Holy Grail, used to collect the blood of the dying Christ. The cup, now sorely worn away, was bequeathed to the estate of the nearby Nanteos family, where it is still guarded. The Welsh can justly complain that the diabolical nomenclature is in any case English, for they themselves call it more sensibly Pont-ar-Fynach, meaning quite simply 'monks' bridge'.

This first bridge has in recent centuries been topped by two more, one above the other, as the road traffic has increased – the three making a unique crowning of a most fascinating rock cleft which is the only access to the beautiful gorge of the Mynach.

The Victorian traveller, George Borrow, like many good travellers, was a raconteur, with an eye for detail and a fine feeling for character, but he was rarely dramatic in his presentation of the beauties and wonders of Wales. However, such was the effect of the scenery around the Devil's Bridge on him that his brief account in *Wild Wales* is quite remarkable: 'Gaze on these objects, namely the horrid seething pot or cauldron, the gloomy volcanic slit, and the spectral, shadowy Devil's Bridge for about three minutes, allowing a minute to each, then scramble

up the bank and repair to your inn, and have no more sight-seeing that day, for you have seen enough. And if pleasant recollections do not haunt you through life of the noble falls and the beautiful wooded dingles to the west of the bridge of the Evil One, and awful mysterious ones of the monk's boiling cauldron, and the long, savage, shadowy cleft, and the grey, crumbling, spectral bridge, I say boldly that you must be a very unpoetic person indeed.'

The third of these three bridges has been added since Borrow's day, so now there is no wild bank to clamber down. Instead there is a slot machine to be fed before pushing through the turnstile to a safe concrete walk. Yet, even such rank tourism has not succeeded in exorcizing the spirit of the place; down by the boiling cauldron, one can forget the turnstiles and the stairs and paths which now make access easy.

This cauldron is actually the largest of a series carved into the rock by the Mynach, just before its waters plunge through the narrow cavities of the gorge, a dramatic cleft some 114 feet deep, framed high above by the three bridges. It is virtually a perpendicular gorge, a mere slit in the black rock face, best seen from the very base near the punch bowl, when winter has gripped the area and the water-flow is snow-charged. The sheer intensity of black and white contrasts is stunning, and at that time of the year both sides of this sentinel to the two wonders – the punch bowl chasm and the six cascades – are electric with a strange intensity which perpetuates the English name for the bridges.

Beyond the bridge, the falls of the Rheidol stream in wild cascades through three hundred feet of almost vertical rocks. It is towards these falls that Wordsworth turned as he stood on the second of the bridges above, and imagined himself at the very beginning of the world. Even a second turnstile, now so expensive to turn, does little to diminish the feeling that there is here something of the pristine wonder which belongs to earlier times.

The largest of the Rheidol cataracts is about 110 feet high, and is usually seen from the safety of the curiously named Jacob's Ladder, which is no ladder but merely a steep stairway from which one might more easily see water undines than angels. It is, in fact, from this stairwell that the most comprehensive view of the falls is possible, yet, for all its size, the serpentine form of the cataracts is partly obscured by foliage, and the best way of enjoying the beauty of the place is by leaving the defined path and making your way to the basins of the individual cataracts, from which five of the main six falls can be contemplated. As with all good things, however, there is an element of danger in this.

Above: A general view of the main falls of the Rheidol, seen from the so-called Jacob's Ladder.

Right: One of the main falls of the Rheidol, which leaps in a series of such cataracts into the deep valley below Devil's Bridge.

Elegug Stacks,
The Green Bridge of Wales,
and St Govan's Head

This part of the south coast comes as a complete surprise . . . wave action is creating fantastic shapes in the carboniferous limestone.
                    P Howell and E Beazley

The Pembrokeshire coastline bravely faces the Atlantic and, as though in a challenge to Neptune, thrusts out a land trident of three rocky prongs. The prong of St David is a dark igneous rock, that of St Anne a red sandstone, while that of the eastern promontory, St Govan, is a hard limestone, partly coloured in dark marl reds. None of these prongs of ancient rock is hard enough to resist forever the pounding of the waves, and the limestone coastline has especially been eroded. The sea has sculpted them all into a wealth of forms, but none more so than at St Govan's Head where a walk of a few miles reveals vertical cliffs, sinuous clefts, caves, arches, chasms and stacks, all superbly set against the booming of the waves and the screaming of sea-birds.

There are few cliffs in the world which exhibit so many different formations within such a short compass as this headland of cliffs below Flimston Downs. Certainly, the Old Man of Hoy is grander by far than any of the stacks of Flimston; the bridges of Flamborough are more rugged than those of this coastline here, and the height of the igneous rocks around Land's End almost dwarfs the cliffs of this Welsh peninsula. Yet each of these three wonders of Britain are separated by hundreds of miles, and here you can find similar formations – only of lesser scale – all within the same short stretch of coast.

The two main stacks of the Elegug rear like frozen leviathans from the sea, and stand off a headland which is still clearly marked with the remains of an iron-age fort. They both have all the delightful properties of sea stacks – the romantic beauty, the visual surprise of the shapes, and the vociferous colonies of sea-birds. If the tank practice in the nearby army practice grounds is silenced for the day along the downs above these cliffs, you can walk to the eroding cliff edge of the downs, and stare at the slim silhouette of the smaller of the two Elegug Stacks a hundred yards or so out in the sea. And if you are there in spring, you will understand

The magnificent Green Bridge of Wales to the west of the Elegug Stacks.

Right: The Elegug Stacks from the north.

why the stacks are so named, for Elegug means 'guillemots', and these sea-birds are here in plenty, squabbling away in the ledges of the stacks which they have made into their own home. There are kittiwakes also, in their cliff colonies, razorbills, and fulmar petrels, and even a few shags, all screaming defiance at the pounding tanks on one side, and at the lashing waves on the other. It seems miraculous that so thin a stalk of limestone as this bird-infested stack should withstand the battering-ram of waves. But then, if you stroll around the top of this small bay, and look once more, another view of the stack presents itself and you see that it is no mere thin pinnacle of limestone, but a huge wedge, solid enough to endure wind and waves for centuries. As for the larger stack, the sculpting by the sea has scarcely begun, for it stands close to the protection of the cliffs, looking firm and solid with its fifty-foot bulk.

From the same viewpoint one need only turn around to feast one's eyes again on the 130-foot drop of the Devil's Punch Bowl – a huge blow-hole and natural bridge combined. On the frequent days of storm, or high waves, the sea pours fury into this blow-hole, and lashes spray into the air over the remains of the ancient fort, smoothing the walls of the natural arch on the sea side of the cavern. From this vantage point

we can step to the right, and see the natural crevices which are daily being widened to extend the blow-hole cavity deeper into the land. We may glimpse the future here: before many centuries have slid by, the whole of this small peninsula will be isolated by the seas, probably to become, at first, a double stack, and later to fall lost beneath the advancing waves.

Peer over these vertical cliffs carefully, for the edges are visibly eroding. At the car-park, on the edge of the military downs, there is a notice informing the public of how many people have been drowned in this area during the past years – four people between 1974 and 1980. Yet the view rewards the prudent observer with boiling seas below, rich varieties of rock formations and subtle hues on their surfaces.

The military signposts which point the motorist to this miracle of cliff sculpture tell only of the 'Stacks', yet to the west of the Stacks is to be found one of the great natural wonders of Wales, a formation which is used again and again in the tourist industry as symbol of the Dyfed coastline – the magnificent Green Bridge of Wales, which edges its warmly coloured arch into the sea off the Flimston Downs.

To the east of the blow-hole is a land-promontory which should delight any geologist, with central strata faults of a sinuous beauty, a backcloth to a play of small stacks, and below, enfolded in the stratification, a wild tumble of rocks and caves which are the hallmark of the Pembrokeshire spectacle.

The path from these spectaculars leads along the edge of the limestone cliffs towards St Govan's Head. It skirts Bullslaughter Bay, the cave-infested cliffs below Crickmail Down and Buckspool Down, to the aptly named Devil's Barn, and then around the impossible 'Huntsman's Leap', once upon a time called 'Adam's Leap', though it is a crevice which never could be leapt by man or beast.

St Govan's itself is an extension of this wildness, a headland which projects further south than any other part of Pembrokeshire. The name is popularly linked with a tiny chapel which mediaeval builders insinuated into a crevice in the cliffs. It is approached from the cliff top, down a rough flight of steps, which in a curious symbolism have one step for every week in the year.

This steep gully of cliffs is rather like a window which looks seaward on to two natural wonders of the inlet. To your left is the almost vertical bridge against which the Atlantic crashes, the foam at times so high as to completely obscure it, the sea no doubt intent on demonstrating how soon it will create a free-

Left: This combined sea-arch and blow-hole, itself a result of the collapse of a cave system, is situated to the east of the Elegug Stacks.

standing stack from this formation. To the right such a stack is already formed. Not so many centuries ago this was also a bridge, yet now it stands guardian to a deep fissure of caves in the limestone rock. The distinctive shape of the column which frames the caves reminds us that many of the stones used in the prehistoric circle at Stonehenge came from Pembrokeshire, the bluestones of the inner circle (so like this column of St Govan's) being transported that vast distance, for reasons which are no longer understood and by means which are still disputed. Beyond this natural standing stone and framed high against the dark limestone bridge is the headland of St Govan's itself.

When you leave the vantage point of the

chapel and scramble down towards the rocks bordering on the sea, you pass the dried-up, though once miraculous, well of Govan, used from about the sixth century by pilgrims. The well appears to have had a curative property, for records tell of sick men healed, of crutches left among the rocks by those who no longer needed them. Legend is sometimes as wild as the cliffs themselves, for the rock-cut cell – which is really a hermitage – is linked with Cofen, who was perhaps the wife of a Welsh king, but there are no historic records. The present building is no later than the thirteenth century, and much restored: the bellcote, viewed from halfway down the steps, is like a man-made stack rearing upwards in competi-

tion with the natural stack standing off the eastern cliffs behind.

It was quite impossible to climb down to the sea level around the Elegug Stacks, to study the wonders from below, but here at St Govan's Head it is possible, and you can make your way to either the bridge or the stack, both of which are best seen at close quarters. Savour the wild beauty of this fantasy of rocks, and then simply turn around to study the rich cliff face behind, with the chapel nestling unobtrusively in the rocks and boulders. Behind you is the lashing sound of waves, above you the screaming of gulls, and before you a wild cliff which Christian saint and centuries of pilgrims have been unable to tame.

Above: The pinnacled arch and sheer cliff face marking the western end of the amphitheatre of rock around St Govan's Chapel.

Far left: A sea-arch marking the eastern end of the same amphitheatre.

Pistyll Rhaeadr

Pistyll Rhaeadr, the finest waterfall of the Welsh Border . . . is visible from a distance of two miles.
William Thomas Palmer

Right: The falls of Pistyll Rhaeadr. Behind the wooden bridge is a small lagoon.

Far right: Pistyll Rhaeadr from the other bank, showing the porthole from which spouts the lower cataract.

Wales is a land of waterfalls, but the greatest of these is Pistyll Rhaeadr on the border of Powys and Clwyd. It was understandably counted by mediaeval writers as one of the 'seven wonders' of the country. The waters leap into the valley a full 240 feet, although they do not make a single leap, which would make them the highest falls in Britain, but a double leap, and it is this which gives Pistyll Rhaeadr much of its unique charm. A close view, which may be had from the left-hand bank of the picturesque gorge, shows the first cataract pouring into a cauldron, and then exploding in a second cataract through a natural bridge which is unique among Welsh waterfalls.

George Borrow, in his quiet and fascinating pilgrimage through Wales and the Welsh language, *Wild Wales*, visited the falls and wrote, 'I never saw water falling so gracefully, so much like thin beautiful threads as here.' His description would suggest that he must have visited the waterfall at one of those rare times in Wales when water was in short supply, for more often the falls are a magnificent cascade which can scarcely be described as thread-like. From certain vantage points, indeed, there is almost something gigantic about the way the first cataract streams over the edge of the cliffs, to disappear behind the trees which line the valley. Such a tremendous view may be had from the road towards Llanrhaeadr-ym-Mochnant: from here there is a sense of scale against the cliffs' ridges and trees which is quite breathtaking. As WT Palmer writes in the *Splendour of Wales*, the falls are visible from a distance of two miles – yet they are best seen from half a mile away, at the top of the incline of the hill road.

There is a crude but quite delightful story attached to the Falls in Chirk Castle, south-east of Llangollen, one of the many ancient Welsh castles open to the public. A large oil painting in the collection there is undoubtedly of Pistyll Rhaeadr, but it shows falls of a prodigious size – perhaps the biggest in the world – for in the

huge lagoon at its base there is a fleet of sailing ships! This was no patriotic boast of a Welsh artist, inordinately proud of his country's wonder, seeking to compare it visually with Niagara, but a linguistic mistake of a Frenchman. It seems that when the French artist had finished the painting, a local Welshman suggested that in order to give it a sense of scale, he might like to include a few 'sheeps' – a suggestion which the Frenchman only too willingly accepted!

This painting, which hangs above the Tudor Staircase in the castle, is of very inferior quality, and it is therefore most surprising to see it officially listed in the catalogue as being by the great Welsh painter Richard Wilson.

Such visual jokes aside, however, Pistyll Rhaeadr is certainly the most lovely of Welsh falls, and the wooded dell into which it crashes is a fitting surround for its beauty. The bridge built to afford a crossing of the river and valley, and no doubt designed to permit safe sightseeing of the falls, does not detract from its beauty. It offers closer access to the further bank, which inclines upwards towards the lower basin of the falls, and makes a natural platform from which one can study the magnificent display to great advantage – even at the expense of a drenching from the spray.

Snowdonia

The Snowdon massif, south of Capel Curig, across the lovely though sullen lake of Lynnau Mybyr.

Like Wales itself, the Snowdonia National Park appears to have no boundaries; its edges are misted over, like so many of its mountain peaks. There are well over eight hundred square miles of park, an area dwarfing the ancient natural fortress of Snowdon itself. The mountains enclosed within are so many eroded stubs of vast rock-folds pressed up by magmatic forces hundreds of millions of years ago, to be smoothed and polished by the rains and ice-flows; they now stretch their boulders south into Cader Idris, from Pormadoc as far as Dyfi Bridge.

Such vastness enfolds many natural glories – the pass of Llanberis, the Conwy valley with its falls, Llyn Tegid, and of course the peaks of Snowdonia, the highest and most beautiful in Wales or England. Few parks in Britain could boast so great a multitude of wonders, such formations to take the breath away, as this Welsh wildness which is marred only by the curved tarmac roads, and the unimaginative serried ranks of Forestry Commission conifers. This is a country of extremes, and if Defoe is wrong, and the Devil does not live in the middle of Wales, then the angels do.

Snowdon is the most famous of wonders set in this wilderness of mountains, surprisingly graced with an English name; the Welsh name for the mountain is *Yr Wyddfa*, probably meaning 'burial place'. It is, like so many Welsh names, unconvincingly explained by reference to the burial of mythological giants. The main peaks gathered around Yr Wyddfa are separated by the Glyders range of mountains, a lovely arc of peaks beloved by mountaineers and walkers, stretching luxuriously in a seven-mile crescent between Bethesda down to Capel Curig, by the Llanberis Pass. The Glyders are numerically superior to the three peaks of Snowdon, for here there are five peaks over three thousand feet, Glyder Fawr, Glyder Fach, Y Garn, Elidir Fawr and Tryfan, ranging from 3,279 feet for the first to 3,010 for the last.

Further north of the Nant Ffrancon Pass are the uplands of Carneddau, with many peaks over the magical 3,000 feet, the highest being Carnedd Llywelyn, closely challenged by Carnedd Dafydd. A vast triad of ranges, yet even these form only a fraction of the many mountains of Wales, and not a single one is so famous or so loved as the peak of Snowdon.

Snowdon and the peak Yr Wyddfa, with the three main supporters of Carnedd Ugain, Y Grib Goch and Y Lliwedd, whose very names are music, present a magical sight. From the top of Snowdon – which is actually reached by a fairly easy climb – on one of those rare clear days in Wales you can see as far as Ireland to the west, over to the Wicklow Hills, and to the north the Isle of Man and the savage mountains of Cumberland.

While Snowdon culminates in the highest peak of Yr Wyddfa – at some 3,560 feet the highest point in Wales and England – it is perhaps best seen when merged with the other nearby peaks of the Snowdonia massif. The finest easily accessible panoramic views are those from the lake Llynnau Mybyr, west of Capel Curig. An hour or so spent in such a place, looking over towards this Snowdon range, will easily dispel the popular notion that mountains are eternal things: the most out-standing quality of any mountain is its very changeability. Mountains don new surfaces, colours, clouds (almost new ridges and peaks in the mutations of light), and offer a bewildering profusion of aspects, as the light changes, the clouds introduce shades, or the rain impercept-ibly etches the forms. From one single vantage point, as from Capel Curig for instance, a thousand photographs of Snowdon taken in a single day could each tell a different story and show a different range of mountains, save in name.

Hidden away in the cwms of the range, sliced out by glacial actions of the Ice Ages long gone, are lakes which still chill in their impressive-ness. In the Green Hollow above Llanberis Pass are the two small lakes protected by Carnedd Ugain. Under Yr Wyddfa is a so-called Green Lake, which does not always look green, but which according to legend hides the awful Afranc monster which once plagued the Conwy. Below lies the Llydaw, the waters of which are poured down the unsightly pipelines that edge their way straight up Snowdon on the Gwynant valley side.

The mountain lakes are beautiful, almost every sheet of water ripples in the imagination with the shades of monsters, or is lightened by the brave deeds of Welsh heroes, each unique in

its beauty, charm or grimness. Most awe-inspiring is Llyn Idwal, 1,223 feet above sea level, which is edged in by the dark and sinister Twll Du, the 'black hole' or the Devil's Kitchen, a cleft in the sheer face of rock. It is said that no bird will fly over its dark surface, because of the terrible death by drowning of Idwal, the son of an early prince of Wales. Few other places in Wales exhibit such stark beauty of natural contrasts of rain and dark.

Ogwen, originally the Ogfanw, high above sea level and a mile long – the source of the rich falls which spume forth under the name of Ogwen to Bwlch y Benglog – is doubtless the very lake into which the sword of Excalibur was thrown by Sir Bedivere for the dying King Arthur, and received by a ghostly hand. Other, more ancient legends surround this lake, its mountain and its river.

In many ways it is from the connection with romance and ancient legend that Snowdon derives its fame, for without such rich historic and mythological associations it would not be, as Borrow so aptly describes it, 'one of the very celebrated hills of the world'. It is as if this wild and unsullied Welsh beauty is so remote as to need a human aspect to make it beloved of humans.

Swallow Falls

The fall at Bettws-y-Coed deserves all the nice things that have been said about it. It is a magnificent cascade.

H V Morton

'The Fall of the Swallow is not a majestic single fall', wrote George Borrow in *Wild Wales*, 'but a succession of small ones. First there are a number of little foaming torrents, bursting through rocks about twenty yards above the promontory, on which I stood. Then come two beautiful rolls of white water, dashing into a pool a little way above the promontory; then there is a swirl of water round its corner into a pool below on its right, black as death and seemingly of great depth; then a rush through a very narrow outlet into another pool, from which the water clamours away down the glen. Such is the Rhaeadr y Wennol, or Swallow Fall; called so from the rapidity with which the waters rush and skip along.'

This is a fine description of a beautiful place, yet, for a man like Borrow with his love of Welsh words, curiously superficial in its explanation of the word 'swallow', for this is seemingly his own guesswork and is inaccurate.

It would be difficult for the average sightseer to work out why the Swallow Falls near Betws-y-Coed should bear their curious name. One might imagine, as did Borrow, that it is the swallow flight of the rapids, or that the idea of a bird may have arisen from a conceit that the dual cataracts represents the two wings of a bird. In fact, the actual explanation for the name is far more romantic than any such guesses would suggest, for it arises from the genius of the Welsh language itself. Originally, the rapids were called *Rhaeadr Ewynol*, 'the foaming fall', and this latter word was corrupted first in sound, and then in orthography, to *y-Wennol*, which means 'of the swallow'.

The waters have hurried down from the mountain range behind Capel Curig and beyond, fed by numerous tiny tributary streams. Their united force breaks over the first of this long series of falls at a point where the river is 60 feet wide, and foams through the rich textures of jagged rocks in the manner described by Borrow: the white streams are sieved

The upper cataracts of Swallow Falls. The white streams recall the legend of a dead soul imprisoned behind the bars of water.

into a whole multitude of teeming cascades.

The roar of this torrent of falls, and the fact that the rock-diverted streams may be fancied as white cage-bars, perhaps explains a popular legend. The locals insist that the spirit of the wickedly avaricious Sir John Wynn (a quite historic personage who died in 1627) is imprisoned within these falls. It is said that his screaming is swallowed up in the roar of the waters, his insubstantial wraith condemned to be washed clean by these peat-filled waters.

The most usual view of the falls is from the railed rampart built on the overhanging rock off the main road. Here one stands on the very same rock upon which George Borrow stood in 1854, and later paid 6d (a lot of money in those days) to the lady who had led him to this spot over the river. Access is nowadays by way of a far cheaper turnstile. Impressive as the view is from this platform, it is at best a partial view, for the falls are about four times higher than they seem from here. Even the climb down a steep stairway which leads to the lower cataract does not give a full view of the falls.

Betws-y-Coed is ideally placed at the junction of the five valleys of the Conwy, the Llugy, Lledr, Machno and the Old Dee, each of which has its own falls and its own special beauties. A little further up river from the Swallow Falls, just before the Machno is captured (to use that delightful technical term beloved of geographers), are the Conwy Falls themselves. The Machno Falls are idyllically placed in a beautiful glen near to an ancient semi-circular bridge, one of the oldest in Wales. Further down are the smaller falls, one of which sometimes takes the form of a white veil of watery mist, and is called with the imagination common to such tourist sights, the 'Bridal Veil'. In the same area, but on the Llugy, is the Miner's Bridge Falls which has a large whirlpool, the Pwll Du, the 'black pool'.

For all that this area around Betws-y-Coed has become a tourist spot, nothing can really dim its enchantment or fully tame its wildness.

Gazetteer

ACHILL ISLAND County Mayo, Ireland. Page 99.
The island is to the north-west of Clew Bay, joined to the mainland of the Curraun Peninsula by way of a bridge over Achill Sound. Keel, from where the Menawn Cliffs may be explored, is on the L141, half way across the island, between the Sound bridge and Achill Head.

AM BUACHAILLE As for STAFFA.
This islet is a few yards out to sea, north-east of the basaltic causeway which leads around to FINGAL'S CAVE. It can be seen a few yards to the south of the normal landing point near CLAMSHELL CAVE.

ARBROATH CLIFFS Angus, Scotland. Page 144.
The town of Arbroath is on the A92, north-east of Dundee. The natural wonders are located along the cliffs which are marked with a nature trail guide, beginning 1 mile to the north-east of the town. See in particular the NEEDLE E'E and the DEIL'S HEID.

BRIDGES OF ROSS County Clare, Ireland. Page 103.
These are signposted to the north of Loop Head, west of Carrigaholt, at the mouth of the Shannon. A visit to the Bridges should be combined with a visit to LOOP HEAD, a mile or so to the south-west.

THE BURREN County Clare, Ireland. Page 104.
The Burren is an area to the south of Galway Bay, perhaps best explored from Ballyvaghan, on the T69. A good and fairly comprehensive circuit tour is by way of Kinvarra on the T69 to Ballyvaghan, then north on the L54 to Black Head (with the main erratics to the north), down to Lisdoonvarna, and back up the T69 to Ballyvaghan, through the finest of the clints. The area is rich in geological and prehistoric wonders, and it is unwise to attempt a survey without a good map and guide, for otherwise the best may be missed.

BUTTERTUBS Yorkshire, England. Page 18.
From the village of Hardraw (see HARDRAW FORCE) take the minor road east for ¼ mile, then turn left, due north, towards Thwaite. This is the Buttertubs Pass, which runs over Abbotside Common. The Buttertubs are signposted to the right of this pass road, about 3½ miles north, at the head of Cliff Beck valley, which opens into Thwaite.

CADER IDRIS Merioneth, Wales. Page 195.
Excellent views of Cader Idris are to be had along the A487 south of Dolgellau. The climb up the Cader to the Lyn Cau is relatively easy. Remain on the A487, driving south as far as Minffordd (about 8 miles south of Dolgellau), then take the minor road fork to the right. A few yards down this minor road, to the right, is an arched entrance to a trackway which begins the path up the Cader, following the descending stream. No special equipment is required for this climb, although strong boots are advisable (about 1½ miles).

CAIRNGORMS Inverness-shire, Scotland. Page 149.
The massif may be seen to advantage from Loch Morlich (see GLENMORE FOREST PARK). Information about ascent and climbing of the peaks can be obtained from the official Information Office to the east of this Loch. There are chairlifts up the Cairn Gorm itself, about 2½ miles south-east of Loch Morlich, reached by signposted minor roads.

CATHEDRAL CAVE See DAN-YR-OGOF CAVES.

CHEESEWRING Cornwall, England. Page 23.
From Launceston take the B3254 south for about 10 miles. Turn right at Upton Cross to the village of Minions (1¼ miles). Just beyond the village outskirts is a right-hand turning down a cart track, signposted to the Hurlers (stone circle), with some adjacent rough parking. Walk along this track through the stone circle (north-north-east) towards Stowe's Hill (about 1 mile). The Cheesewring is first seen on the further side of the quarry, to the south of this hill, and can be approached along a path around the left-hand edge of the quarry.

CLAMSHELL CAVE As for STAFFA.
This cave is north of the basaltic causeway. The most frequent sea-landings are made almost at the entrance to the cave, but, if you land in the north, a walk directly across the turf along the eastern edge of the cliffs (almost 1 mile south) leads to the cave. It is best seen from sea-level, from the hexagonal stubs of basalt to the north of the entrance.

CLIFFS OF MOHER See MOHER.

DAN-YR-OGOF CAVES Powys, Wales. Page 198.
From Sennybridge (on the A40 between Brecon and Llandovery), drive south on the A4067 for about 11 miles. The caves (including the Cathedral Cave) are signposted to the right, a few yards off the road, 750 yards north of Craig-y-nos castle, with ample parking before the entrance.

DEIL'S HEID As for ARBROATH CLIFFS.
This formation is nearly a mile north along the cliff edge nature trail, on a wide rock promontory to the right, jutting into the sea.

DEVIL'S BRIDGE Dyfed, Wales. Page 202.
Devil's Bridge is on the A4120, about 13 miles east of Aberystwyth and about 3 miles south of Ponterwyd. The parking is inadequate during tourist seasons.

DEVIL'S CAULDRON As for LYDFORD GORGE.
The Cauldron lies at the end of the signposted walk through the Gorge, beneath the road bridge, and therefore within easy reach of the main entrance. Final access is by way of a swing-plank bridge, and is perhaps not for the infirm.

DEVIL'S PUNCHBOWL As for DEVIL'S BRIDGE.
The Punchbowl is approached by way of a pay-turnstile, to the right of the bridge.

DONEGAL See ERRIGAL.

DOVER Kent, England. Page 27.
Dover lies at the termination of the A2 from the London direction. The cliffs surrounding Dover, and within easy reach, are the Shakespeare Cliff to the west and the series of white cliffs stretching along to St Margaret's Bay, both of which can be explored on foot along the signposted walks, or (more difficult) along the shingle and rocks of the beaches. But see also ST MARGARET'S BAY.

DUNCANSBY STACKS Caithness, Scotland. Page 153.
Take the A9 towards John O'Groats, and shortly before entering village turn along the (signposted) minor road to the east for Duncansby Head lighthouse, which is on the coast (1½ miles) with parking to the left. The stacks are about 1 mile south along the coastal paths (signposted at the beginning).

DUNNOTTAR FIDDLEHEAD
Kincardineshire, Scotland. Page 157.
The castle of Dunnottar, which is on a peninsula served by the Fiddlehead, is signposted on the right of the A92, 1 mile south of Stonehaven. Parking is off this main road, alongside gatehouse, with a walk of ¼ mile to the peninsula.

DURDLE DOOR Dorset, England. Page 70.
From Wool on the A352, drive south along the B3071 for 4 miles, then continue south on the B3070 for 1 mile to West Lulworth. There is ample parking to the right of this road, as one arrives in the village at the head of the Cove. Behind the carpark is a signposted walk of about 1 mile to the Durdle Door, along the cliffs of Dungy Head and St Oswald's Bay (due west). The Durdle Door is to the west of the headland spur, beyond St Oswald's Bay, descent to which is by way of rather steep stairs.

ELEGUG STACKS Dyfed, Wales. Page 207.
From the village of Castlemartin, on the

B4319 towards Pembroke and about 1 mile east, turn south through Flimstone and continue along the signposted road towards 'Stacks'. A short walk from the ample car-park along the cliff top, due east, leads to stacks, arch and blow-hole. Since this part of the Pembrokeshire coastline is approached through tank-training grounds, the roads are often closed to traffic: opening times are clearly displayed daily. The cliffs are steep, eroding and dangerous, and visitors are publicly advised to exercise great care. There is a fine walk of approximately 3 miles from the Stacks, east along the coastline to St Govan's Chapel.

ERRIGAL County Donegal, Ireland. Page 112.
The mountain is to the north of Dunlewy, on the L82, some 18 miles north-west of Letterkenny.

FINGAL'S CAVE As for STAFFA.
Fingal's Cave pierces the southern tip of the island and is approached by way of the basaltic pavement from the usual landing place opposite Clamshell Cave (less than ¼ mile walk due south).

FIONNPHORT As for MULL.
Fionnphort is 37 miles west of Craignure at the end of the A849, which serves the Iona Ferry, on the Ross of Mull.

FLAMBOROUGH HEAD Yorkshire, England. Page 31.
From Bridlington take the A165 north for 1 mile, turn right at the B1255 and continue 4½ miles to Flamborough village. Parking about 1½ miles roughly equidistant from the village at Thornwick Bay (ample parking) or Selwicks Bay, both signposted.

GAP OF DUNLOE See KILLARNEY

GIANT'S CAUSEWAY County Antrim, Ireland. Page 116.
The Causeway is well signposted to the north of the A2, about 6 miles east of Portrush. Parking at the National Trust car-park, where excellent maps of the area's natural phenomena are on open public display.

GLENCOE Argyll, Scotland. Page 160.
The Pass of Glencoe is on the A82, starting about 14 miles north of Tyndrum. Glencoe itself is to the south of Loch Leven. The drive along the Glen is just over 7 miles, with adequate parking at the official Information Centre, to the right of the top end of the Glen.

GLENMORE FOREST PARK
Inverness-shire, Scotland. Page 149.
From Aviemore take the A951 east for 1½ miles to Coylumbridge, then continue east on a minor road for about 3½ miles, roughly following the River Luineag, to Loch Morlich. Parking space to both the west and east of the Loch.

GORDALE SCAR Yorkshire, England. Page 34.
From the village of Malham (see MALHAM COVE), take the signposted minor road east to Gordale Bridge (1 mile), which offers limited roadside parking. Walk north from this bridge, then across footpath to the left, to continue along the stream of Gordale Beck, which leads in about ½ mile to the entrance of the Scar.

GREEN BRIDGE OF WALES As for ELEGUG STACKS.
The natural arch of the Green Bridge is a few hundred yards east from the car-park, along the coastline.

HARDRAW FORCE Yorkshire, England. Page 18.
From Hawes, on the A684, take left turning north across Brown Moor on the minor road to Hardraw (1½ miles). Access to the Force is through the pay-kiosk at the *Green Dragon* inn, the falls themselves being ½ mile up the valley beyond.

HENHOLE Northumberland, England. Page 38.
From Kelso, on the A698, take the B6352 for 7 miles to Town Yetholm, then drive 1 mile south on the B6401 and take the first left fork down a minor road. Continue on this minor road (alongside Bowmont Water) to Swindon (about 5 miles) and south-east to Cockslawfoot (2 miles), where the road terminates. Park near the ford opposite a farm, then take a poorly marked footpath across Cheviot Burn towards north-east headlands until you arrive at the well-marked footpath along the eastern edge of College Valley, from which the Henhole can be observed. It is unwise to attempt this journey without a 1:50000 metric Ordnance Survey Map (Sheet 74, *Kelso*, gives Henhole at 885201; Sheet 80, *The Cheviot Hills*, gives Cockslawfoot at 855185).

HIGH FORCE Durham, England. Page 42.
High Force is on the B6277, 5 miles north-west of Middleton in Teesdale, from where it is signposted. There is ample paking to the right of the road, just before a hotel. Access to the falls via a pay-kiosk, on the opposite side of the road. A walk of about ½ mile leads directly to the falls.

HOLY ISLAND See LINDISFARNE.

KILLARNEY County Kerry, Ireland. Page 122.
Killarney is a tourist town, centred on a junction with the T67, the T29, the T30 and the T65. For a good view of the lakes take the T65 south to the east of Lough Leane, and some 6 miles on to Muckross Lake. This road continues along to Ladies' View (signposted). The Gap of Dunloe is signposted south, on the T67, 5 miles west of Killarney.

LAND'S END Cornwall, England. Page 46.
The A30 terminates at Land's End, transformed into a short minor road which feeds the vast tracts of parking with traffic. The finest views are from the cliffs to the east of the headland.

LINDISFARNE Northumberland, England. Page 50.
From Berwick on Tweed take the A1 south for 8 miles to West Mains, then turn left towards Beal (signposted), and it is 1½ miles to Holy Island Sands. Near and during high tide, crossing of the causeway is prohibited. At low tide take the causeway 1 mile to the Snook; the road curves round the south of the island along a causeway (further 2 miles) to village, where there is ample parking.

LOCH LOMOND Stirlingshire/ Dunbartonshire, Scotland. Page 164.
The Loch stretches to the east of the A82 from Balloch, 3 miles north of Dumbarton, up to Ardlui. A fine view of Ben Lomond is to be had from the A82 at Tarbet (parking). A trip on the *Maid of the Loch* (the last of the British paddle steamers) from Balloch gives an excellent view of the many islands. Inchailloch is opposite the Garadhban Forest at Balmaha (parking).

LOGAN STONE Cornwall, England. Page 54.
From LAND'S END take the first turning right off the A30 (B3315) to Trethewey, which is some 3½ miles via Polgigga. Turn south to Porthcurno (¾ mile), to ample parking on the left. Across this parking area, take the signposted coastal road to the eastern peninsula where the rock is situated. The walk to the Logan Stone along the peninsula involves a degree of climbing, and stout shoes should be worn.

LOOP HEAD County Clare, Ireland. Page 127.
The Head is at the end of the signposted minor roads which continue on from the L51 beyond Kilkee. The Dermot and Granias Rock is to the west, beyond the lighthouse; the sea-arch, to the north of the road, is approximately ½ mile before the lighthouse. Extreme caution must be observed while exploring these dangerously steep cliffs.

LYDFORD GORGE Devon, England. Page 57.
Take the A386 south of the A30 beyond Okehampton. The village of Lydford is signposted to the right, about 6 miles south. The Gorge runs under the minor road which bisects the far end of the village, and a few yards to the right, beyond this bridge, is the National Trust entrance, with adequate parking. The walk along the Gorge is about 2½ miles (just over a mile between DEVIL'S CAULDRON and the WHITE LADY).

MALHAM COVE Yorkshire, England.
Page 60.
From Skipton take the A65 west, through Gargrave to Coniston Cold (about 7 miles), then turn right (due north) on a minor road to Airton (3 miles) and continue on to Malham, north of Kirby Malham (2½ miles in all). Park at the Information Centre to the left and walk up Cove Lane behind the Centre. The Cove is visible to the right, a few hundred yards up the lane, but is a further ¾ mile across the valley. The clints of Malham are best approached by way of the left-hand pathway (part of the Pennine Way) up to the top of the Cove.

MOHER County Clare, Ireland.
Page 109.
The long stretch of cliffs are well sign-posted on the L54, 7 miles south-west of Lisdoonvarna. The signs direct one to the tourist car-park, from which the conventional views and walks may be conducted. Walks, both south-west and north-east, to the two extremities of the cliffs, give breathtaking views generally not explored by tourists.

MULL Argyll, Scotland. Page 169.
The island is served by a number of fairly frequent ferries from the Scottish mainland, the two main ones being that from Oban to Craignure (taking about 45 minutes) and that from Lochaline to Fishnish (taking about 8 minutes). See also FIONNPHORT.

NEEDLE E'E As for ARBROATH.
This formation is about ⅓ mile along the cliff nature trail, to the right.

NORBER ERRATICS Yorkshire, England. Page 65.
The village of Clapham is left of the A65, between Ingleton and Settle. Park in the village (Information Centre) and walk along Thwaite Lane, entry by way of bridge to the north of the village. This lane leads to Austwick. The Norber clints are on top of the outcrops about ¼ mile to the left of Thwaite Lane, above Thwaite Scar and Robin Proctor's Scar. The erratics are almost at the end of Thwaite Lane, to the left across rough pasturage, and below the Robin Proctor's Scar.

OLD HARRY ROCK Dorset, England.
Page 69.
From Northport take the A351 about 4½ miles south-east to the junction with the B3351, which is left at Corfe Castle. Continue on this road, for about 5 miles to the village of Studland. From the village walk along a marked pathway due east to the Foreland, nearly a mile beyond the village. Old Harry Rock is the stack off the tip of the point, best seen from the headland to the west.

OLD MAN OF HOY Orkneys, Scotland.
Page 172.
The Scrabster ferry on the north coast of Scotland goes to Mainland, Orkneys, landing at Stromness. From here there is

an infrequent boat to Linksness, on the island of Hoy. From Linksness pier take the B9047 south for 1 mile until the signposted minor road to Rackwick (about 3½ miles). The Old Man stack is about 2 miles north-west of Rackwick and is reached by way of a longer walk up and around Moor Fea, or along the cliffs of Rora Head. The infrequency of boats, and the distances involved, generally require that at least one night be spent on Hoy (hostel facilities are available), although a taxi service is usually available between Linksness and Rackwick. It is not advisable to make a journey to the Old Man (and especially along the top of the cliffs of St John's) without a good Ordnance Survey map.

PEAK CAVERN Derbyshire, England.
Page 72.
Peak Cavern lies to the south of the village of Castleton, which is on the A625. Access to parking is signposted. The cavern is entered by way of the cleft below Castle Hill, at the edge of the village, and is signposted.

PISTYLL RHAEADR Powys, Wales.
Page 212.
From the quiet village of Llanfyllin, take the B4391 north for 2 miles to the junction with the B4580, and then follow this road for a further 3 miles to Llanrhaeadr-ym-Mochnant. The falls of Pistyll Rhaeadr lie some 4½ miles along the valley road, to the north-west of this village. Sign posts lead to a car-park, unobtrusively sited near the edge of the falls basin.

RHEIDOL FALLS As for DEVIL'S BRIDGE.
The Rheidol Falls are approached by way of a pay-turnstile, to the left of the bridge. A steep hair-pin pathway and stairs lead down towards the basin, and then up the other side of the valley, alongside the cascades, ending in front of the hotel at the head of the falls.

ROCHE Cornwall, England. Page 75.
From Bodmin take the A30 south-west for about 6½ miles. The village of Roche is signposted to the left, on the B3274, just over 1 mile south. The rock outcrops, marked on the Ordnance Survey map as 'Roche Rocks', are on the southern side of the village, to the right of the minor road signposted to Bugle.

ROCK CLOSE County Cork, Ireland.
Page 131.
The Close is signposted, in the grounds of Blarney Castle, 5 miles north-west of Cork.

ST GOVAN'S HEAD Dyfed, Wales.
Page 207.
From the village of Bosherston, 1 mile south of Sampson (on the B4319 from Pembroke), a road leads directly to a car-park near St Govan's Chapel, which is set in a cleft, with the small sea-stack to the west, the natural arch to the east and the magnificent headland sweep of St

Govan's Head on the eastern coastline. The latter may be approached by foot along the coastline below Trevellen Down (about ½ mile from the car-park).

ST JOHN'S HEAD As for OLD MAN OF HOY.
The spectacular cliffs of St John's Head are about 2 miles north of the Old Man and 3 miles west of Linksness, but a walk through this difficult terrain involves greater distances (especially in wet weather, which is remarkably frequent in Hoy), and should not be undertaken without an Ordnance Survey map (Sheet 7: *Pentland Firth*, 1:50 000).

ST MARGARET'S BAY Kent, England.
Page 27.
From DOVER take the A2 north to the first roundabout, then turn right onto the A258 (towards Deal). After ½ mile turn right along the B2058 to St Margaret's at Cliffe. Parking is alongside the main shingle beach. There is a fine walk from Dover along the shingle of Langdon Bay, Fan Bay and on to St Margaret's Bay.

ST MICHAEL'S MOUNT Cornwall, England. Page 78.
The Mount is off the coast at Marazion, on the A394 between Helston and Penzance, about 3 miles east of the latter. Crossing to the Mount is by boat at high tide, by causeway at low tide.

SEVEN SISTERS Kent, England.
Page 80.
Drive west from Eastbourne on the A259 for 7½ miles. Just before Sutton (about ½ mile after descending to the road bridge over the Cuckmere River) turn left along minor road for ¾ mile (signposted). Park on top of South Hill. Walk about ½ mile due east, along signposted pathways to cliff on western side of Cuckmere Haven for panoramic view of the Seven Sisters.

SKELLIGS County Clare, Ireland.
Page 135.
These rock islets rear out of the Atlantic about 7 miles west of Bolus Head, at the south-western tip of the Iveragh Peninsula, and are usually approached by boat from Valentia Island (the pier opposite the Royal Hotel). Bad weather, and landing difficulties caused by the swell, make it impossible to ensure daily trips. When at all possible, the boat trip takes about 1½ hours and is not always comfortable. One can stay on Skellig Michael for just over two hours, on Little Skellig not at all, save under extraordinary circumstances.

SNOWDONIA Gwynedd, Wales.
Page 212.
A fine panorama of the Snowdonian massif may be had on the A4086, south-west of Capel Curig. A steady climb to the peaks starts to the north-west of the A498 at Nantgwynant, but there are many climbs of various degrees of difficulty, and the general traveller is advised to obtain local guidance from Infor-

mation Centres (Llanberis or Blaenau Ffestiniog, for example).

STAFFA Argyll (Inner Hebrides), Scotland. Page 179.
This island may be visited by way of tourist excursions from Oban, from Ulva or from Dervaig on the island of MULL. Unfortunately, some of the commercial firms will carry tourists to see the island when the weather is far from suitable, and it is advisable to make such a trip only when the weather and the forecast promise well. Private trips may be arranged from the island of Iona, which is itself reached via the ferry on Mull (see FIONNPHORT). Due to the unpredictability of the Atlantic, landings on Staffa are rarely guaranteed by experienced seamen – though a landing is essential to savour the full beauty of this island. Landing is usually at the concrete jetty by CLAMSHELL CAVE, which is joined to the famous FINGAL'S CAVE by the basaltic causeway; however, I have been landed during heavy swell on the rocks to the north-east of the island.

SWALLOW FALLS Gwynedd, Wales. Page 218.
From Betws-y-Coed take the A5 north for about 3 miles. The falls are signposted to the right, with ample parking to the left, in front of the hotel. Access to the falls is by way of a pay-kiosk.

TREAK CAVERN Derbyshire, England. Page 83.
Treak Cavern is about ¾ mile out of Castleton, west on the A625, and is signposted to the left of this road, to the north of WINNATS PASS. Parking at the side of the road, or in the ample car-park a few hundred yards back up the A625, before the entrance to Winnats.

WHITE LADY FALLS As for LYDFORD GORGE.
The falls are to the western end of the gorge and may be approached directly from the minor entrance to the gorge from the Lydford-Tavistock road, or as the culmination of the gorge walk, which starts from the main entrance to the National Trust building and car-parks.

WHITE SCAR CAVES Yorkshire, England. Page 87.
From Ingleton, on the A65, take the B6253 north-east for about 1½ miles. The cave entrance, with ample parking, is clearly displayed to the right of the road, beneath the swell of White Scar itself.

WINNATS PASS Derbyshire, England. Page 83.
West of Castleton on the A625, take the first left-hand fork, towards the signposted Pass, which begins just beyond the kiosk entrance to Speedwell Cavern. Parking to the right.

YESNABY CASTLE Mainland, Orkneys, Scotland. Page 185.
Stromness, the main port of Mainland, is reached by ferry from Scrabster on the northern coast of Scotland. Take the A965 north for 1½ miles, then the A967 for a further 3 miles north, veer left for a few hundred yards on the B9056, then left on the signposted minor road for 1½ miles to Yesnaby. The stack is signposted, about half a mile to the south, along cliffs towards Brough of Biggin.

Glossary

BASALT A dark igneous rock of complex structural form, most often found in columnar vertical stratifications.

BLOW-HOLE A conduit from the upper part of a cliff to a lower point, which permits the sea to burst through it.

CALCITE The main constituent of limestone – calcium carbonate. Found also in stalactites and stalagmites.

CAMBRIAN A period at the very beginning of the Palaeozoic era, some 600 million years ago.

CARBONIFEROUS A period related to the formation of coal strata in the earth, starting some 270 million years ago.

CLINT A clint is actually a hard or flinty rock, but the term is frequently used in connection with the 'clint pavements' of limestone rocks which are characterized by deep fissures (see GRYKES). The formations are a result of water erosion.

CLOCHANS Beehive-shaped stone huts, found especially in Ireland where these monastic structures first appear about the sixth century AD.

CONGLOMERATE A sedimentary rock composed of round pebbles held in a natural cement.

CORRIE A circular hollow or depression on a mountainside.

CWM Deep hollow or valley in a mountainside.

ERRATIC An erratic is a displaced boulder, usually carried from its original site as part of glacial detritus during the Ice Ages.

FAULT A fracture in the structure of a rock.

GEO A geosynclinal depression is a large hollow in the surface of the earth, with a steady and gradual rise to either side. The term geo is used in a general and popular sense for a long fissure or channel in the earth or in rocks.

GNEISS A slate-like granite; a metamorphic rock with a laminate structure.

GRYKES The name given to the fissures which traverse and criss-cross the limestone pavements of CLINTS. The deep channels or grykes are worn into the limestone by the acidic action of rainwater.

KARST Rough limestone country with underground drainage.

MAGMA The semi-fluid igneous substance normally located below the surface of the earth's crust.

MARL A clay-like soil, mixed with carbonate of lime.

METAMORPHIC ROCKS A wide variety of rocks, formed during times of great stress in the earth's crust, in which the original sedimentary or igneous rocks are subjected to change from intense heat and/or pressure.

OUTLIER In a geological sense an outlier is an area of young rocks surrounded by older rocks. However, the same term is used to denote standing stones which lie outside the main circle of a prehistoric ring.

PHYLLITE A rock consisting of a slate containing flakes of mica.

PLUTON A rock extrusion created by volcanic activity. Pluto was the Roman god of the underworld.

POTS Deep holes formed by the erosion of running streams.

PRECAMBRIAN A period that comes before the CAMBRIAN, but does not have defined dates.

SCHIST A type of crystalline metamorphic rock.

SILL A bed of rock, especially of an intrusive igneous variety.

STACK A column of rock detached from its parent cliff by the action of the elements, especially the sea.

STALACTITES A calcite deposit, icicle-like in structure, hanging down from the roof, or down the sides of caves.

STALAGMITES A calcite incrustation standing upright on a cave floor, formed by drips from the roof.

TURLOUGH A depression which, due to the nature of the supporting rocks or limestone, fills with water through crevices during periods of rainfall, but empties during dry periods.

Bibliography

Anderson, JGC 'Glenmore' in *Cairngorms*, edited by John Walton, Edinburgh 1966

Bailey, Patrick *Orkney* Newton Abbot 1971

Banks, FR *The Peak District* London 1975

Bates, Darrell *Devon and Cornwall* London 1976

Borrow, George *Wild Wales: Its People Language and Scenery* London 1920

Boswell, James *Journal of a tour to the Hebrides*, edited by Lawrence F Powell, London 1957

Burton, JH *The Scot Abroad* Edinburgh 1864

Clark, Sir Kenneth *Landscape into Art* London 1979

Coase, AC *Official Guide to the Cathedral Cave* (n.d.)

Davidson, Robin *Cornwall* London 1978

Defoe, Daniel *Tour through the whole island of Great Britain (1724)* London 1975

Drabble, Margaret *Writers' Britain: Landscape in Literature* London 1979

Gaunt, Arthur *Discovering Yorkshire* Tring 1970

Gower, Edward *Flamborough: A Guide for Visitors* Clapham 1979

Hammond, RJW *The Peak District* London 1978

Hardy, Thomas *The Hand of Ethelberta* London 1876

Hillaby, John *Journey Through Britain* London 1968

Howell, Peter and Beazley, Elisabeth *South Wales* London 1977

Kazantzakis, Nikos *England* Oxford 1972

Lehane, Brendan *Ireland* London 1973

Lindsay, Maurice *By Yon Bonny Banks* London 1961

Linklater, Eric *Orkney and Shetland* London 1980

Llewellyn, Alun and Vaughan-Thomas, Wynford *Wales* London 1969

MacCulloch, Donald Brown *Staffa* Newton Abbot 1976

MacMahon, Bryan *Here's Ireland* London 1971

Mais, SPB *The Unknown Island* London 1932

Mais, SPB *I Return to Ireland* London 1948

Molyneux, T *Transactions of the Royal Society* Vol. 18, London 1964

Morton, HV *In Search of Wales* London 1952

Mould, Daphne Pochin *The Mountains of Ireland* Dublin 1976

Mowat, Bill *John O'Groats* Caithness 1964

Murray, William Hutchinson *West Highlands of Scotland* London 1977

Newby, Eric and Petry, Diana *Wonders of Ireland and How to Find Them* London 1969

Norway, Arthur H *Highways and Byways in Yorkshire* London 1899

O'Brien, Kate *My Ireland* London 1962

O'Faolain, Sean *An Irish Journey* London 1940

Palmer, William Thomas *The Splendour of Wales* London 1932

Philipson, J *Northumberland National Park* London 1969

Plunkett, James *The Gems She Wore: Book of Irish Places* London 1978

Raistrick, Arthur *Malham and Malham Moor* Clapham 1976

Retler, Wolfgang *Ireland Explained* London 1966

Robinson, Tim D *The Burren: A Map of the Uplands of N.W. Clare, Eire* Kilronan 1977

Rodgers, Peter R *Geology of the Yorkshire Dales* Clapham 1979

Rose, Harold *Your Guide to Ireland* London 1965

Royse, John *The Geology of Castleton* London 1904

Rynne, Stephen *All Ireland* London 1956

Scott, Harry J *Portrait of Yorkshire* London 1970

Selincourt, Aubrey de *The Channel Shore* London 1953

Seymour, John *South East Coast of England* London 1975

Simpson, WD *Dunottar Castle. Historical and Descriptive* Aberdeen 1976

Steven, Campbell R *Enjoying Scotland* London 1971

Turner, James *The Stone Peninsula* London 1975

Waltham, AC *White Scar Caves* (n.d.)

Wordsworth, Dorothy *Tour in Scotland in 1803* Edinburgh 1973